Redefining Teacher Preparation

Redefining Teacher Preparation

Learning from Experience in Educator Development

Edited by Caroline M. Crawford
and Sandra L. Hardy

ROWMAN & LITTLEFIELD
Lanham • Boulder • New York • London

Published by Rowman & Littlefield
A wholly owned subsidiary of The Rowman & Littlefield Publishing Group, Inc.
4501 Forbes Boulevard, Suite 200, Lanham, Maryland 20706
www.rowman.com

Unit A, Whitacre Mews, 26–34 Stannary Street, London SE11 4AB

Copyright © 2017 by Caroline M. Crawford and Sandra L. Hardy

All rights reserved. No part of this book may be reproduced in any form or by any electronic or mechanical means, including information storage and retrieval systems, without written permission from the publisher, except by a reviewer who may quote passages in a review.

British Library Cataloguing in Publication Information Available

Library of Congress Cataloging-in-Publication Data Is Available

ISBN 978-1-4758-3917-3 (cloth: alk. paper)
ISBN 978-1-4758-3918-0 (pbk: alk. paper)
ISBN 978-1-4758-3919-7 (electronic)

∞™ The paper used in this publication meets the minimum requirements of American National Standard for Information Sciences—Permanence of Paper for Printed Library Materials, ANSI/NISO Z39.48–1992.

Printed in the United States of America

Contents

Foreword *Nancy P. Gallavan*	vii
Preface	xi
Acknowledgments	xv
Editors' Note *Caroline M. Crawford and Sandra L. Hardy*	xix
Introduction *Caroline M. Crawford and Sandra L. Hardy*	xxi
Overview and Framework *Caroline M. Crawford and Sandra L. Hardy*	xxv
1 Classroom Teachers as Associated Teacher Educators: Applying ATE Standards for Teacher Educators *Romena M. Garrett Holbert and Robert Fisher*	1
2 Context Is Everything: Increasing the Relevance of Preservice Teachers' Experiences in Classroom Management *Benjamin R. Wellenreiter*	23
3 Becoming Teacher Educators: Transformational Journeys of Classroom Teachers *Nancy P. Gallavan*	41
4 Learning from Experience: Insights from Veteran Classroom Teachers on Teacher Preparation *Louise Ammentorp*	59

5 Classroom Teachers as Associate Teacher Educator
Perspectives: Framing Dialogues and Professional
Development Contexts among Professional Educators 75
Caroline M. Crawford

Afterword 95
Caroline M. Crawford and Sandra L. Hardy

About the Editors 99

About the Contributors 101

Foreword

Serving as the president of the Association of Teacher Educators (ATE) includes the privilege of appointing one or two Commissions to guide the association with topics and issues in education. This privilege is accompanied with the responsibility of identifying particular areas of importance and/or concern as well as inviting interested members to participate on the Commissions.

Commissions allow ATE members to meet regularly to discuss research and practices followed by opportunities to disseminate presentations and publications. By delving into multiple perspectives associated with a particular area and deliberating the impact on teacher education, Commission members help inform and support both the actions of ATE and contribute to the research literature grounding teacher education.

The ATE Commission on Classroom Teachers as Associated Teacher Educators is one Commission that I joyously appointed in 2013 as I began my ATE presidency. My vision for this Commission was to consider the research and resources available to classroom teachers and that ATE can promote combined with the technological avenues that ATE can establish to strengthen the educational preparation of our vital partners in teacher education found in the field.

I greatly value the expertise of classroom teachers, the energies they dedicate to their learners, and the experiences they provide in the preparation of classroom teachers; appointing this Commission allowed me to empower and equip teacher educators both at universities and in classrooms. Establishing this Commission sparked the conversations to revisit the origin of ATE and the contributions to education given that ATE began in 1920 as the National Association of Directors of Supervised Student Teaching.

I believe that teacher education involves the aligned messages, modeling, methods, and mentoring from two significant sources: (a) expert university instructors and well-developed courses in teacher education and (b) experienced P-12 teachers and classrooms in a variety of content subject areas, educational settings, and diverse communities. Sound research and accrediting agencies have long rationalized that teacher preparation requires strong partnerships between university instructors and classroom teachers.

My aim was to select a group of ATE members ascribing to this belief. Plus, my own career resonates the reciprocity shared between the university and the classroom; I have evolved from an undergraduate education candidate who prepared to be a classroom teacher, an intern in the classroom, a novice teacher, a graduate student teacher leader, a classroom intern mentor, and a doctoral candidate to a teacher educator, an intern supervisor, and a teacher educator preparing future doctoral teacher educators. Therefore, appointing this ATE Commission was a natural reflection of my life's work and meaningful decision for the ATE.

For many years, educators have faced an unresolved dilemma in teacher preparation. Many teacher preparation personnel and programs grapple with the dynamics involved in their partnerships with school administrators and classroom teachers. Likewise, many school administrators and classroom teachers wrestle with the expectations in their partnerships with universities and interns.

Everyone agrees that new classroom teachers must be prepared by qualified teacher educators for ever-changing educational contexts. However, only through a seamless partnership specifying the purposes of each participant in the preparation of teachers will the intern, P-12 learners, classroom teachers, educational systems, and teacher preparation benefit.

As an educator who has evolved from a classroom teacher to a university instructor, I am fully aware of one overarching concern. Frequently, when classroom teachers are asked to mentor a university teacher preparation intern, the classroom teachers do not view themselves as teacher educators nor do they approach mentoring as an opportunity contributing to their personal growth, professional development, and pedagogical expertise.

Too often, classroom teachers respond to the request to mentor interns as another task consuming their time, energy, and sometimes, their money. Revisiting the purposes and practices of a seamless partnership between the teacher preparation program and the P-12 school poses five specific benefits for the classroom teacher that may influence teacher preparation processes and outcomes.

BENEFIT ONE

While mentoring a university teacher preparation intern, the classroom teacher has the rare opportunity to view individual practices through the eyes of another professional in a nonthreatening environment. Few professions offer this type of chance to reflect critically on one's own practices then to modify and advance practices appropriately. Most teachers think about improving their practices as if someone were watching; mentoring an intern transforms thoughts into authentic outcomes.

BENEFIT TWO

While transforming thoughts into authentic actions, the classroom teacher can develop mechanisms to enhance teacher self-efficacy. Most classroom teachers who are asked to mentor an intern demonstrate proficiencies to guide and support an apprentice. These proficiencies indicate that the classroom teacher has developed the confidence and competence to affect and promote student learning with comfort and care for the learner and the teacher. The opportunity to mentor an intern encompasses the optimal professional development.

BENEFIT THREE

While optimizing professional development, the classroom teacher also has the opportunity to transform personal growth and pedagogical expertise. As a mentor, the classroom teacher may realize the individual benefits from the passage of time and the discoveries from experience. These insights provide the intern with the most valuable perceptions that the intern will glean and take into her or his own career. The keen classroom teacher recognizes these unique and astute moments for one generation to shape future generations.

BENEFIT FOUR

While shaping future generations, the classroom teacher not only gains in pedagogical expertise, but the classroom teacher also increases acumen into andragogical practices. University interns are adults aspiring to become classroom teachers. Although the classroom teacher mentor and the university intern are focused on advancing their pedagogical expertise to increase the engagement and achievement of their students, the relationship between the mentor and the intern centers on anagogical practices related to the teaching, learning, and schooling of adults.

Knowles (1980, 1984) identified five characteristics of andragogy essential for the education of adults: (a) adults are moving from dependency to self-directedness; (b) experiences accumulate into resourcefulness; (c) readiness to learn is oriented as developmental tasks of social roles; (d) perspectives change from postponed or future use to immediate application accompanied with a shift from subject centeredness to problem centeredness; and (e) motivation becomes internal rather external.

BENEFIT FIVE

Consequently, while experiencing the transformation of the intern, the classroom teacher is also experiencing transformation in ways that benefit the teacher, the students, the school, and the community. Many classroom teachers who mentor interns discover new horizons in education prompting them to pursue additional endorsements, advanced degrees, and new career choices such as university teacher educators. Unlike the teaching, learning, and schooling associated with P-12 students, mentoring interns offers classroom teachers with new, perhaps endless, possibilities. I certainly can attest that this series of transformations influenced my career.

CONCLUDING THOUGHTS

I am excited that the members of the ATE Commission on Classroom Teachers as Associated Teacher Educators have authored this text. Shepherded by the Commission Text co-chairs, Caroline M. Crawford and Sandra L. Hardy have assembled a fascinating collection of outstanding research and principles applicable to teacher preparation, professional development, and learning communities.

These insightful chapters provide well-developed purposes and practices contributing to the roles, responsibilities, and rigor of classroom teachers who mentor interns in their transformation as teacher educators and partners in the preparation of teachers. I greatly appreciate the dedication of this text's coeditors and all of the authors who have contributed to its success.

—**Nancy P. Gallavan,**
Association of Teacher Educators President 2013–2014

REFERENCES

Knowles, M. (1980). *The modern practice of adult education: From pedagogy to andragogy*. Wilton, CN: Association Press.
Knowles, M. (1984). *Andragogy in action*. San Francisco, CA: Jossey-Bass.

Preface

The Association of Teacher Educators (ATE) Commission on Classroom Teachers as Associated Teacher Educators is a professional community focusing upon the professional development needs of classroom teachers as associated teacher educators. A classroom teacher who takes on the role of an *associated teacher educator* is a quality professional who focuses additional time, effort, and subject matter expertise upon supporting and training pre-service teacher candidates, novice teachers, as well as experienced colleagues within and across the field-based classroom environments.

Professional standards and dispositions are applied within real-world classroom engagement. While working closely with teachers, administrators, and university-based instructors, classroom teachers also take on the added responsibilities to work with teacher candidates. In this leadership role, classroom teachers may be named associated teacher educators. The associated teacher educator is the classroom teacher who holds significant skills and abilities including, but are not limited to, a level of subject matter expertise; an understanding of the curricular design and student learner cognitive needs, instructional prowess within the current K-12 classroom experiential needs; as well as dispositional understandings and the ability to assess the teacher candidates and support novices as well as more experienced educators across real-world settings working with university teacher educators.

The ability to effectively embrace K-12 classroom teaching while supporting teacher candidates, novice and experienced colleagues is a role that deserves further exploration and recognition. Thus, the classroom teacher as teacher educator is the three-text set's central focus and is presented in three distinct but related text's themes. Each area of focus is discussed and further defines classroom teachers as associated teacher educators.

The first text, *Redefining Teacher Preparation: Learning from Experience in Educator Development*, highlights applications and reflections of Association of Teacher Educator (ATE) Standards and offers conceptual frameworks and contextual realities in connections to classroom educators at all stages of their career.

The second text, *Dynamic Principles of Professional Development: Essential Elements of Effective Teacher Preparation,* focuses upon differentiated elements toward inquiry and the reflectivity of practitioners as dynamic components of professional development.

The third text, *Teacher to Teacher Mentality: Purposeful Practice in Teacher Education*, focuses upon professional discourse that revolves around induction efforts resulting from educators working together to inform one another's practice.

ATE is a professional community focusing upon redefining teacher preparation to promote advocacy, equity, leadership, and professionalism through learning from experience in educator development. Therefore, ATE promotes classroom teachers as associated teacher educators across settings to achieve quality education and collegial collaboration for all learners.

An understanding of the ATE Commission on Classroom Teachers as Associated Teacher Educators may be framed through the innovative efforts of Dr. Nancy Gallavan, ATE past president, as her insightful vast understandings of teacher education transformations led to the realization of this Commission.

The ATE Commission on Classroom Teachers as Associated Teacher Educators (active from 2013 through 2016) has been productively engaged in enriching discussions and cutting-edge efforts, not only through a theoretical and research focus but also through the attainment of classroom teacher input. As such, it is appropriate to reflect the Commission's efforts through the availability of this three-text set of texts that reflect the current state of classroom teachers as associated teacher educators while promoting avenues for future developments in this regard. Thus, the text reflects the Commission's vision and mission while promoting avenues for future developments in this regard.

COMMISSION VISION

The ATE Commission on Classroom Teachers as Associated Teacher Educators promotes advocacy, equity, leadership, and professionalism for classroom teachers as associated teacher educators in all settings and supports quality education and collegial support for all learners at all levels and contexts.

COMMISSION MISSION

The ATE Commission on Classroom Teachers as Associated Teacher Educators advocates quality teacher education through exemplary collaborative efforts and collegial understandings that reflect the inherent importance of classroom teachers as associated teacher educators.

As ATE past president Nancy Gallavan (2013–2014) has described the charge of the ATE's Commission on Classroom Teachers as Associated Teacher Educators to include the consideration of the research and resources available to classroom teachers. Further the Commission's mission recognizes that ATE promotes, combined with the technological avenues, the ATE establishment of informative and supportive vital educational preparation of partners in the field.

With the esteemed group of Commission colleagues that Dr. Gallavan coalesced, the Commission brings forward meaningful ideas for projects, research endeavors, publication efforts, as well as considerations toward enhancing grant funded areas of focus. The Commission also paves pathways toward further establishing ATE as a primary resource through which to obtain high-quality professional development opportunities, with special emphasis upon classroom teachers who also mentor and guide teacher candidates, novice classroom teachers, and colleagues.

Acknowledgments

CAROLINE M. CRAWFORD

There are so many colleagues who have been involved in the success of this text. I would like to first acknowledge the Association of Teacher Educators (ATE) as a truly extraordinary professional organization. The professionals within this organization live, breathe, and forever journey through strengthening the profession of teacher education. Through the ATE, I have been honored to meet, work with, and forever have been impacted by truly extraordinary teacher educators, who have supported my understandings within the field as well as developed a sense of a welcoming family among our ATE membership.

I would like to begin this discussion through an acknowledgment of my deep respect and collegial admiration for Dr. Nancy P. Gallavan. Her trust and belief in my abilities led to this opportunity to chair the Association of Teacher Educators (ATE) Commission on Classroom Teachers as Associated Teacher Educators that occurred from 2013 through 2016. These 3 years were an amazing experience and quite a learning journey, for which I will always be grateful.

I would also like to bring forward my appreciation for our many colleagues who engaged in our Commission on Classroom Teachers as Associated Teacher Educators as committee members who engaged in our mission quite selflessly. Each committee member brought forward their own professional strengths, qualities, and pleasant creativity as we progressed forward toward realizing our Commission's successes. The strength of understanding and depth of respect for professional classroom teacher colleagues was inherent in each undertaking and realized within each of the Commission's successes.

I would like to state my respect for the amazing talents that each of our Committee Member colleagues brought forward toward supporting our mission, as well as the thoughtful efforts recognized within each demanding undertaking. The Commission membership has every reason to reflect a level of accomplishment throughout our Commission experience, as our years together have not only strengthened our professional understandings but also added fundamental and essential work to the professional knowledge base.

I would also like to acknowledge and deeply thank Dr. Sandra L. Hardy for being such an integral part of our text as an integral coeditor, as well as fundamentally important in our Commission's success. Thank you for always being professional, amazingly supportive, always going so far above and beyond all of my hopes for support, and for reflecting your true self as a proficient, skilled, knowledgeable, generous, kind, and caring professional. This text would not have been realized without your depth of engagement throughout our journey.

A truly amazing faculty advisor, mentor, and ultimate teacher educator is a rare gem of a professional. This describes Dr. Allen R. Warner, professor emeritus, from the University of Houston in Houston, Texas, USA. I still find it difficult to describe the deeply professional and personal impact that I have been honored to experience as I reflect upon my doctoral studies, tenure-track faculty years and as a tenured faculty member within the higher education university environment. Dr. Warner must be acknowledged as a true academic scholar and a true teacher educator.

Throughout my doctoral studies, Dr. Warner represented the faculty advisor guidance, patience, and benevolent oversight that developed my true understanding of the profession as one worthy of the highest esteem. Even after so many hours, days, months, and years of sacrificing his own time and effort toward supporting his students, the only request has been to *pass it forward* and impact others as profoundly as Dr. Warner impacted my own professional understanding and career path. I imagine that Dr. Warner may never know the true depth and breadth of his impact upon his students and colleagues, but I want to ensure this small acknowledgment highlights his truly significant career.

Finally, I would like to acknowledge the quality of university students with whom I have been honored to work. The undergraduate and graduate students with whom I have worked over the decades are exemplary examples of what I consider to be the best and the brightest within academia.

Students with whom I have been honored to work come from innumerable realms, including PreK–12 education systems as classroom teachers and professional staff, business and industry, medical education, higher education, and so many associated venues within which teaching, training, and instructional design quality support the vision and mission of the organizations.

I learn just as much from my learner colleagues as what I share, and for this reinvigorating energy, creativity, innovation, and sense of community, I am forever grateful.

SANDRA L. HARDY

The completion of the Commission on Classroom Teachers as Associated Teacher Educators three texts—*Redefining Teacher Preparation: Learning from Experience in Educator Development; Dynamic Principles of Professional Development: Essential Elements of Effective Teacher Preparation; Teacher to Teacher Mentality: Purposeful Practice in Teacher Education*—was made possible because of the diligent work ethic and dedication of so many individuals. I would like first and foremost to express immense gratitude to the Association of Teacher Educators (ATE) for bringing together a multitude of educators at all levels of the spectrum from preservice teachers through college deans.

ATE supports on so many levels the professional development of teachers, administrators, and teacher educators at all stages of their career and provides the opportunity to come together and learn from one another on a local, state, national, and international scale. ATE is also an organization that fosters teacher leadership. It is through the dynamic leadership and keen insight of former ATE president, Dr. Nancy P. Gallavan, that our Commission on Classroom Teachers as Associated Teacher Educators came to fruition. Thank you, Dr. Nancy P. Gallavan.

Our commission was further enriched by the exemplary leadership of Dr. Caroline M. Crawford as commission chair. Dr. Crawford, also the coeditor of the afore mentioned books, time and again went far above and beyond the duties of chairing the commission to ensure that each member had ample opportunities to both express their ideas and unleash their full potential as commission members, members of the teaching profession and learning communities.

Further, Dr. Caroline M. Crawford served as an amazing mentor to me throughout the entire editing process. With Dr. Caroline M. Crawford's steadfast leadership we rose time and again above and beyond tremendous challenges and recognized the importance of details to keep the texts moving forward. For all this and so much more, I am deeply thankful to Dr. Caroline. M. Crawford.

I pause at this juncture to recognize two outstanding teacher educators who influence and serve the education community in an exemplary fashion, Dr. D. John McIntyre and Dr. Christie McIntyre. Dr. D. John McIntyre, former ATE president, was also the chair of my doctoral committee as well as one of my teacher educators. Dr. D. John McIntyre serves as a shining example of an outstanding teacher educator, administrator, researcher, author, and editor. Dr. McIntyre provides encouragement and guidance to doctoral students and brings the long arduous journey of their dissertation to a successful defense.

Dr. Christie McIntyre, current ATE president for the Illinois State chapter, early childhood teacher educator, researcher, and role model for teacher educators, also contributes to doctoral students educational programs and committees, and serves the education communities in so many ways in her support to teachers, students, and as a model to teacher educators both in the university classroom and in the field as well as in to the learning communities. Thank you, Dr. D. John McIntyre and Dr. Christie McIntyre.

I would also like to express my sincere gratitude to each and every individual who contributed their work to the content of our commission's written works. Without their giving selflessly of their professional knowledge, skills, abilities, and time the completion of these endeavors would not have been possible. Each author, as well as each assistant and associate reviewer, is a shining example of the education profession in their area of expertise. The culmination of these many individual professional teacher educators brought forth collectively the fruition of our Commission's efforts that will further serve to enrich the teaching profession and bring insight and support to many teachers across the teaching continuum for years to come. Thank you to all those teachers who made our mission a reality.

In closing, I embrace this opportunity to extend a heartfelt expression of gratitude to all of the truly dedicated professional educators who work tirelessly with compassion to make a difference in the life of so many individual teachers and learners in more ways than they may ever know. I further acknowledge with appreciation the multitude of learning communities who provide the support networks and link resources for teachers as learners and teacher educators to collaboratively improve their practice as they progress with renewal in all stages of professional development. Some of these educators participated in the completion of these texts, and some are a part of the research that is written about in the chapters.

Many are the educators who will find knowledge and support through the reading, discussion, and application of the content in the three texts brought forth by the Commission of Classroom Teachers as Associated Teacher Educators on behalf of the Association of Teacher Educators.

Editors' Note

Caroline M. Crawford and Sandra L. Hardy

The editors would like to thank the hard work and extensive efforts of their reviewers.

EDITORIAL ADVISORY BOARD OF REVIEWERS

Associate Reviewers: Book Chapter Manuscript Reviewers

The significant impact of the text associate reviewers was truly appreciated. Dr. Billi Bromer, Dr. Caroline M. Crawford, Dr. Nancy Gallavan, Dr. Sandra L. Hardy, and Dr. Jennifer Young extended their professional time, effort, and expertise toward carefully reviewing and offering detailed feedback throughout the second round of book chapter double-blind reviews.

The editors would like to extend their heartfelt appreciation for these professionals who were able to extend themselves beyond the bounds of normal expectations of realistic quality and timeliness. Careful book chapter manuscript reviews were achieved within short time periods, and the detailed quality of support and engagement by each associate reviewer was impressive. For this, we, Dr. Crawford and Dr. Hardy, express our sincere appreciation.

Assistant Reviewers: Book Chapter Proposal Reviewers

The initial double-blind peer review efforts of the submitted proposals for this text's journey were extensions of professional creativity and innovation and were innumerable. The professional efforts and expertise of their assistant reviewers brought forward the strengths of each proposal, for which Dr. Crawford and Dr. Hardy would like to state appreciation to Dr. Billi Bromer, Dr. Lynda Cavazos, Dr. Caroline M. Crawford, Dr. Sandra L. Hardy, Dr. Lisa Huelskamp, and Dr. Nancy Gallavan.

They were integrally important, very much valued, respected, and each professional is highly esteemed for their depth of review effort. The high quality and impact of this text would not have been realized without the assistant reviewer's initial strength of effort. For this, Dr. Crawford and Dr. Hardy offer significant thanks.

Introduction
Caroline M. Crawford and Sandra L. Hardy

This text is meant as a reflection of the current *state of the profession* as it revolves around the concept of classroom teachers as associated teacher educators. This text serves also as a tool for promoting professional discourse concerning redefining teacher preparation in learning through experience pertaining to the development and implications of classroom teachers as associated teacher educators. This is such an important discussion to be had, and yet only recently has the teacher education profession more fully realized, acknowledged, and emphasized the integral impact of classroom teachers as associated teacher educators in this regard.

Such dynamic interchanges extend to teacher candidates, novice classroom teachers, and teacher educators. Further, these promote the continued excitement and innovative creativity necessary and appropriate for all of our classroom educators in order to attain and exhibit consistent displays of subject matter expertise, and an inherent understanding of the learning communities that integrates nuanced understandings associated with differentiated learning landscapes. These shared understandings and expertise as well as the ability to embrace lifelong learning coupled with resources serve to fuel the excitement of transformations found in professional renewal.

The enriched key points in the three texts highlight and integrate differences within the realm of teacher education through the theoretical, data-driven, and contextual realities of teaching and learning. These underpinnings are then the basis of the transformational journey toward becoming classroom teachers and teacher educators that also benefit veteran teachers in the process.

The texts are designated into three separate, yet related, areas of focus:

- *Redefining Teacher Preparation: Learning from Experience in Educator Development*
- *Dynamic Principles of Professional Development: Essential Elements of Effective Teacher Preparation*
- *Teacher to Teacher Mentality: Purposeful Practice in Teacher Education*

Each text engages in intriguing frames of discussion from various regional areas of the United States of America. Furthermore, the chapters contained in each text explores the different types of school districts and parishes, including shifts from large metropolitan independent school districts and those pertaining to smaller towns and principalities that support and engage in teacher education field-based efforts.

One of the core strengths of the teacher education profession is the integral, continuous, and highly respected field-based classroom educators who formally and informally serve as associated teacher educators. Each of the texts extends and links the rich discourse beyond the bounds of the academic hallways into the teachers' classrooms, highlighting the amazing work efforts, professional dispositions of continuous engagement, nurturing efforts, and amazingly demonstrated professionalism as displayed by classroom teachers in their roles as associated teacher educators and in working with university-based faculty in this regard.

The first text is titled *Redefining Teacher Preparation: Learning from Experience in Educator Development*. The chapters highlight applications and reflections of the Association of Teacher Educators (ATE) Standards for Teacher Educators and offer conceptual frameworks and contextual realities in connections to classroom educators at all stages of their career as associated teacher educators.

The transformational nature of the teacher education process reflected in these chapters reflects a deeper understanding of the professional shifts of theory and practice dynamics within and across school district as well as university-based teacher educators. These partnerships provide vast opportunities for professional development to learn and share through contextual engagement and communication of differentiated roles and associated experiential journeys that result in enriched practice and reflection as shared throughout the authored chapters.

The text *Dynamic Principles of Professional Development: Essential Elements of Effective Teacher Preparation* focuses upon differentiated elements toward inquiry and the reflectivity of practitioners as dynamic components of professional development. The chapters explore the sense of professional development that often occurs within the context of the field-based classroom experiences and school sites, while still allowing for a metaphoric dance that represents the deep connectivity linked to more formalized professional development opportunities.

Such opportunities include the sharing of experiences and engaging of useful instructional outcomes, as well as discourse that occurs among professional educators. These elements extend beyond the conceived ivory tower and are further integrated within the learning landscape of practice that is the pre-kindergarten through 12th-grade school districts and teachers' classrooms' environmental venues.

Hence, the chapters in this text illustrate classroom teachers as associated teacher educators engaged in powerful and effective mentorships and collegial support networks within and across contexts of learning and learning how to teach. These integral processes are further intricately interconnected within multiple levels of influence and engagement that reflectively results in a continuing dialogue of understanding and impact that connects learning communities to improve practice as evidenced in the authored chapters.

The text *Teacher to Teacher Mentality: Purposeful Practice in Teacher Education* focuses upon professional discourse that revolves around induction efforts and highlights dispositional understandings associated with effective teacher leaders. These elements as well as teacher candidate collegial support by classroom teachers are also explored in the chapters.

These key concepts integrate and form the basis of effective collaborations between teacher candidates, classroom teachers, field-based university supervisors, and teacher education faculty that resonate in the chapters. An intriguing shift within this text are the dispositional underpinnings as framed through communities of learning, communities of practice (Wenger, 1998, 2009) as well as Wenger's more recent learning in landscapes of practice (Wenger-Trayner, Fenton-O'Creevy, Hutchinson, Kubiak, & Wenger-Trayner, 2015).

This text is offered to serve as a guiding framework that is adjustable as a useful tool toward developing and transforming pathways in meeting the professional development needs of the individual classroom teacher as associated teacher educators. It is important to emphasize that this framework has moveable components and therefore shifts to suit various contexts and levels of teacher development, including those paradigms of teacher educators at the university and beyond.

The following chapters further reflect the development of an approach toward professional understanding and professionalism of teacher educators within and across all levels and contexts of teacher education discourse and engagement.

REFERENCES

Wenger, E. (1998). *Communities of practice: Learning, meaning, and identity*. Cambridge, MA: Harvard University Press.

Wenger, E. (2009). A social theory of learning. In K. Illeris (Ed.), *Contemporary theories of learning: Learning theorists . . . In their own words*. New York, NY: Routledge.

Wenger-Trayner, E., Fenton-O'Creevy, M., Hutchinson, S., Kubiak, C., & Wenger-Trayner, B. (2015). *Learning in landscapes of practice: Boundaries, identify, and knowledgeability in practice-based learning*. New York, NY: Routledge.

Overview and Framework
Caroline M. Crawford and Sandra L. Hardy

Teacher preparation and contexts of understanding are inherently fraught with flowing shifts and understandings in approaches toward teacher preparation and contexts of conceptualizations. Over the decades, efforts toward supporting teacher preparation have delved into community-focused, field-based programs of study, shifting toward classroom-based training that emphasized theories and models.

These programs then speedily shifted back toward a field-based approach within laboratory schools and true field-based approaches that emphasized not only the theoretical and model understandings but also the practical bases that are emphasized within real-world classroom experiences. Within these movements and paradigm shifts, the classroom teachers as associated teacher educators have never wavered in importance.

Although the vast majority of university faculty and field-based instructional supervisors have backgrounds in pre-kindergarten through 12th-grade classroom teaching experience, the complexity of the classroom environment continues to change over time. This complexity consists of several key elements including, but not limited to, the changes of ongoing technological advancements, and the call for increasing academic achievements in a regional, state, as well as global context.

Within this context, with an expanding diversity of students' and their unique learning needs, it is important to recognize that there is a greater pressure to raise their academic performance even in schools where adequate resources such as funding for personnel and supplies may be restricted. Therefore, the most appropriate person to bridge the gap between learned understandings and real-world, site-based efforts are the classroom teachers who give of their time and expertise as associated teacher educators.

Experiential learning is at the heart of the teacher education and preparation construct, emphasizing contextual frameworks toward understanding the teaching and learning process. Experiential learning theory (Kolb, 1984; Kolb & Kolb, 2008) was built upon the foundational understandings of Kurt Lewin (1935, 1936, 1948, 1951; Lewin & Grabbe, 1945; Lewin & Lippitt, 1938; Lewin, Lippitt, & White, 1939) and John Dewey (1997, 2004, 2005 and 2008) and other integral theorists.

Experiential learning "offers a dynamic theory based on a learning cycle driven by the resolution of the dual dialectics of action/reflection and experience/abstraction" (Kolb & Kolb, 2008, p. 42). Within this environmental understanding, the learners engage in transformational journeys, or transactional events, within the teaching and learning environments.

From a journeying metaphor, one may recognize the transformation that occurs as one's teacher education path embeds experiential understandings and reflective practices within the surrounding support systems of experienced teacher educators as well as teacher candidate colleagues. As teacher candidates journey through a landscape of practice, conceptual frameworks of understanding as framed by Vygotsky (1933/1966, 1935, 1978, 1981; Barwell, 2015; Esteban-Guitart, 2015; Metraux, 2015; Montealegre, 2016; Wang, 2015) are more fully developed.

Vygotsky's work helped frame the teacher candidate's journey. However, this journey through a landscape of practice is tested and reflected upon as the theoretical and student-based experiential understandings evolve to develop more fully within the shifts that occur from a student perspective toward a professional classroom teacher educator orientation.

Garrett Holbert and Fisher begin this text with a discussion revolving around the Association of Teacher Educators' Standards for Teacher Educators entitled "Classroom Teachers as Associated Teacher Educators: Applying ATE Standards for Teacher Educators." These standards offer explanatory and dispositional elements revolving around the roles of teacher educators within our schools as well as within and across university environments. The ATE effort is toward informing and guiding teacher educators so as to focus upon quality distinctions and associated professional efforts.

Wellenreiter in chapter 2, "Context Is Everything: Increasing the Relevance of Preservice Teachers' Experiences in Classroom Management," brings forward a conversation that centers the importance of context within teacher candidate experiences, with special attention toward classroom management understanding and engagement. His emphasis focuses upon the deeply engaged analytical understandings and reflective efforts by the teacher candidates, with special attention toward the contextual analyses of student behaviors within contextual bounds.

The emphasis upon understanding the school community and analyzing different classroom management concerns must be based within a clear understanding of the school site, the behavioral norms within the student body, and within the classroom student makeup. Engaging activities that focus upon contextual understandings also bring forward implications for teacher education programs of study.

Gallavan, in "Becoming Teacher Educators: Transformational Journeys of Classroom Teachers," focuses her discussion in chapter 3 on the transformational journey that each of us as classroom teachers travels, in supporting teacher candidates toward becoming classroom teachers. An intriguing statement begins the discussion, framing an understanding that highly qualified classroom teachers may not have received the preparation or support necessary in the process of becoming mentors for teacher candidates.

How many classroom teachers have shared stories of their busy mornings, getting ready for a full day of experiences with their classroom full of students, and then enjoy a surprise visit from the school administrator? This administrator quickly shares that you will enjoy a new teacher candidate addition to your class for the next 12-week period, and the teacher candidate will show up in the next 15 minutes.

This timeless story has been shared all too often. As the teacher candidate's journey begins in the classroom teacher's field-based placement, both colleagues learn and grow together; the teacher candidate learns and develops into a classroom teacher, and the classroom teacher miraculously evolves into a mentor with strengthened understandings of experiential and modeling efforts who transforms within a self-efficacy–based understanding of oneself into recognition of self as an associated teacher educator.

Ammentorp leads our fourth chapter, "Learning from Experience: Insights from Veteran Classroom Teachers on Teacher Preparation," within this text's discussion, framing experiential learning and the associated professional reflections of a veteran classroom teacher's insights into teacher preparation. This is an integrally important chapter, as so many voices can be lost in the focus upon teacher preparation programs, curricular engagement, and state-mandated standards to be directly aligned and addressed.

These voices all lead toward the state's teacher licensure examination successes and attainment of one's own classroom in which to begin a professional career path within which to positively impact so many children, colleagues, and community. The discussion emphasizes the significance of associated with teacher educators remaining grounded within school communities and resulting implications that support reciprocal and collaborative relationships.

Crawford champions our fifth chapter, "Classroom Teachers as Associate Teacher Educator Perspectives: Framing Dialogues and Professional

Development Contexts among Professional Educators." She engages in a discussion of the initial foray of the Commission on Classroom Teachers as Associated Teacher Educators, through the representation of the primary themes and subthemes that arose from a qualitative study effort early in the Commission efforts.

The qualitative survey of classroom teachers, both novice and veteran, as well as student candidates and student teachers, leads to insightful findings. This chapter is a transformational journey, not only due to the expected thematic findings within the chapter but also the unexpected and forthright feedback received.

REFERENCES

Barwell, R. (2016, July). Formal and informal mathematical discourses: Bakhtin and Vygotsky, dialogue and dialectic. *Educational Studies in Mathematics 92*(3), 331–345.

Dewey, J. (2008, January). Experience and education. *The Educational Forum, 50*(3), 241–252. Retrieved from http://dx.doi.org/10.1080/00131728609335764

Dewey, J. (1997). *How we think*. Mineola, NY: Dover Publications, Inc.

Dewey, J. (2004). *Democracy and education*. Mineola, NY: Dover Publications, Inc.

Dewey, J. (2005). *Art as experience*. New York, NY: Penguin Group.

Esteban-Guitart, M. (2015). LS Vygotsky and education by Moll, LC: (2014). New York, NY: Routledge, 173 pp. *Journal of Language, Identity & Education, 14*(4), 295–297.

Kolb, A. Y., & Kolb, D. A. (2008). Experiential learning theory: A dynamic, holistic approach to management learning, education and development. In S. J. Armstrong & C. Fukami (Eds.) *Handbook of Management Learning, Education and Development* (pp. 42–68). London: Sage Publications.

Kolb, D. A. (1984). *Experiential learning: Experience as the source of learning and development*. Englewood Cliffs, NJ: Prentice-Hall, Inc. Retrieved from http://academic.regis.edu/ed205/kolb.pdf

Lewin, K. (1935) *A dynamic theory of personality*. New York, NY: McGraw-Hill.

Lewin, K. (1936) *Principles of topological psychology*. New York, NY: McGraw-Hill.

Lewin, K. (1964). *Field Theory in Social Science: Selected Theoretical Papers*. New York: Harper & Row.

Lewin, K., & Grabbe, P. (1945). Conduct, knowledge, and acceptance of new values. *Journal of Social Issues, 1* (3), 53–64. doi: 10.1111/j.1540-4560.1945.tb02694.

Lewin, K., & Lippitt, R. (1938). An experimental approach to the study of autocracy and democracy. A preliminary note. *Sociometry, 1*, 292–300.

Lewin, K., Lippitt, R., & White, R. (1939). Patterns of aggressive behaviour in experimentally created "social climates". *Journal of Social Psychology, 10,* 271–299.

Métraux, A. (2015). Lev Vygotsky as seen by someone who acted as a go-between between eastern and western Europe. *History of the Human Sciences, 28*(2), 154–172.

Montealegre, R. (2016). Controversias Piaget-Vygotski en psicología del desarrollo [Piaget-Vygotsky controversies in developmental psychology]. *Acta Colombiana de Psicología*, 19(1), p. 271–283.

Schermerhorn, R. A. (1948). *Resolving social conflicts. Selected Papers on Group Dynamics*. By Kurt Lewin. In G. W. Lewin (Ed.), Resolving social conflicts; Selected papers on group dynamics. Social Forces, 27 (2), 167–168. New York: Harper and Brothers. doi: https://doi.org/10.2307/2572316

Vygotsky, L. (1978). *Mind in society: The development of higher psychological processes*. Cambridge, MA: Harvard University Press.

Vygotsky, L.S. (1933/1966). Play and its role in the mental development of the child. *Soviet Psychology*, 12(6), 62–76.

Vygotsky, L. S. (1935). *Mental development of children during education*. Moscow-Leningrad: Uchpedzig.

Vygotsky, L. S. (1981). The genesis of higher mental functions. In J. V. Wertsch (Ed.), *The concept of activity in Soviet psychology*. Armonk, NY: Sharpe.

Wang, R. (2015). LS Vygotsky and education. *British Journal of Educational Studies*, 63(1), 112–114.

Chapter 1

Classroom Teachers as Associated Teacher Educators

Applying ATE Standards for Teacher Educators

Romena M. Garrett Holbert
and Robert Fisher

ABSTRACT

Effective preparation of new teachers and the continued growth of practicing teachers require collaboration across traditionally defined categories of educators. Collaborations between classroom-based teacher educators employed in schools and teacher educators employed by universities take on a wide variety of forms and evidence inconsistency in valuation of classroom teachers' influence on educator development.

The Association of Teacher Educators (ATE) has developed Standards for Teacher Educators which describe roles of teacher educators in schools and universities. This chapter focuses on intersections between the standards and the work of classroom teachers as associated teacher educators.

KEYWORDS

Classroom teacher as associated teacher educator, collaboration, cultural competence, primary teacher educator, professional development, program development, public advocacy, scholarship, standards for teacher educators, teacher education profession, teaching, vision

> Teacher educators are identified as those educators who provide formal instruction or conduct research and development for educating prospective and practicing teachers. Teacher educators provide the professional education component of preservice programs and the staff development component of inservice programs.—"Why the Standards?", Task Force on Standards for Teacher Educators

Teacher educators take on varying levels of formalized responsibility for the professional learning of preservice and practicing teachers. Teacher educators who have responsibility for program design, development, and implementation of educator preparation programs will be referred to as primary teacher educators. Other personnel enact significant roles within teacher education programs by leveraging roles associated with their employment as resources for teacher development. For example, a reading methods instructor (either campus or school based) is likely to be a primary teacher educator.

A classroom teacher who is chosen to be a model of reading instruction uses his or her employment as a P-12 educator to enhance professional learning of educators, and thus is appropriately termed an associated teacher educator. Classroom teachers as associated teacher educators are a pivotal force in the professional education of preservice and practicing teachers.

In recent years developments in teacher education have increased the potential for classroom teachers as associated teacher educators to enact significant roles within teacher education programs. Many classroom teachers provide instruction or supervision of clinical experiences of prospective teachers. Classroom teachers also take on essential professional education roles with practicing teacher colleagues as curriculum coaches, department heads, mentors, and coaches to support the successful completion of professional assessments associated with annual teacher evaluation and licensure renewal.

Classroom teachers who take on such roles centered on administration or delivery of instructional activities that support professional study for teachers are also associated teacher educators. Much research documents classroom teachers' contributions noting that they spend the most time with student teachers (Osunde, 1996), model and provide feedback on instructional practice (Graham, 2006), and play powerful roles in shaping teacher candidates' instructional materials and dispositional characteristics (Anderson, 2007).

The increased expectations for the roles of associated teacher educators in the initial and continuing education of teachers led the Association of Teacher Educators (ATE) to create a Commission on Classroom Teachers as Associated Teacher Educators. The charge to the Commission was to identify and reflect upon the roles of associated teacher educators. This text is one result of their work. In this chapter, the Standards for Teacher Educators developed by

ATE will be highlighted with special emphasis on the role of the classroom teacher.

HISTORY AND DEVELOPMENT OF THE STANDARDS FOR TEACHER EDUCATORS

Twenty-five years ago, the ATE, the one organization that focuses on teacher educators' role in the education of teachers, began the bold initiative of defining that role. The Commission appointed to this work, led by Dr. Robert Houston, immediately discovered the lack of research and writing about teacher educators. It is appropriate to mention that this initiative coincided with the publishing of the first compendium of research on teacher education (Houston, Haberman, & Sikula, 1990). These and other initiatives mark the major thrust in professionalizing the role of the teacher educator.

Also at this time was an increase in partnerships between higher education and schools in the initial preparation and continuing education of teachers. Early drafts of the new teacher educator standards were seen as focusing more on the role of the teacher educator in higher education. Subsequent revisions broadened the wording, indicators, and artifacts to reflect the role of school-based teacher educators.

The second issue that arose was calling the work *standards* (Clift, 2009). Although the original motivation for the work was to set standards to distinguish those engaged in teacher education, the use of the document proved more to be an *operational definition* to enable all who engage in teacher education to grow professionally.

That is, no matter what level of engagement and expertise one has as a teacher educator there is room for improvement. In particular, a classroom teacher who hosts a student teacher now has a guide to becoming more effective in that role. The value of the document has been demonstrated in the development of those engaged in teacher education rather than measuring a specified level of achievement. Examples of such use include self-reflection by teacher educators and design of programs that prepare teacher educators.

NINE STANDARDS FOR TEACHER EDUCATORS

In the sections that follow, each of the Standards for Teacher Educators is stated and then briefly articulated and linked to the roles, responsibilities, and role-related capacities of classroom teachers as associated teacher educators. Selected actions which evidence classroom teachers' strong command of each standard are advanced at the conclusion of each section. Descriptions of each standard as they apply across multiple teacher educator identities and contexts as well as artifacts which may document accomplished professional practice surrounding each standard are available on the ATE website at http://www.ate1.org/pubs/uploads/tchredstds0308.pdf.

Standard 1—Teaching. *Model teaching that demonstrates content and professional knowledge, skills, and dispositions reflecting research, proficiency with technology and assessment, and accepted best practices in teacher education.* Classroom teachers as associated teacher educators model related practices for preservice and practicing teachers. Integrating their work as P-12 teachers and teacher educators, classroom teachers as associated teacher educators have expanded opportunities to demonstrate, provide rationales for, clarify, and assist in the development and analysis of teaching practices which focus on what is best for individual students as learners.

For example, classroom teachers as associated teacher educators play powerful roles in shaping the learning of preservice and practicing teachers toward enactment of best practices. These teacher educators support classroom teachers' abilities to enact learner-centered teaching through provision of modeling during learner-centered professional development during which teachers focus on student work as evidence and utilize collaborative problem solving. Learner-centered teaching practices emphasize complex problem solving and higher-order thinking skills (Bransford, Brown, & Cocking, 2000; Cornelius-White, 2007).

Such practices have been identified as bridging well-documented achievement gaps (Cornelius-White, 2007) and providing for students to actively construct meaning from experiences relating to their prior knowledge (Lawless & Pellegrino, 2007). Implementation of learner-centered instruction requires teachers to develop deep understandings of their students and to develop and refine pedagogical approaches such as modeling and questioning which enable classroom students to build upon their prior knowledge (Penuel, Fishman, Yamaguchi, & Gallagher, 2007).

In practice, classroom teachers may demonstrate their practice in relation to teaching through the layering of practice in which they make positive impacts on student learning not only by means of directly teaching students for whom they serve as the teacher of record, but also by influencing the practice of future or current teachers. Teaching adults involves different strategies than teaching children. Andragogy, the teaching of adults, emphasizes that adults approach learning in a need-to-know basis.

Among others, actions taken by classroom teachers as associated teacher educators which evidence strong command of Standard 1 include: modeling instruction that meets the needs of diverse students and teacher candidates; promoting critical thinking and problem solving among teachers and prospective teachers; revising classroom-based actions and educative experiences to simultaneously meet the needs of P-12 students and the educators who serve their learning needs; and, grounding their interactions with students and educators in current policy, research, and outcomes of reflection.

Standard 2—Cultural Competence. *Apply cultural competence and promote social justice in teacher education.* Classroom teachers as associated teacher educators can directly model the value and power of in-depth understandings of self and students, families, and communities on instructional outcomes. Classroom teachers accomplished in the area of cultural competence embrace the imperative advanced by Moll, Amanti, Neff, and Gonzalez (1992) to recognize and value students' "cultural funds of knowledge"—arrays of resources available to teachers and students which stem from students' households.

These teachers also understand the lived curriculum as experienced by their students and transcend stereotypes to evidence valuation of individual students' uniqueness and multiple identities (Aoki, 1993). Through their own classroom practice, and their facilitation of reflection upon preservice and practicing teachers' enacted practices, classroom teachers as associated teacher educators promote inquiry into differences such as culture, religion, gender, native language, sexual orientation, and varying abilities and developmental levels.

Intersecting with their roles as advocates, accomplished classroom teachers not only make connections to students' experiences, but also "teach all students the implicit rules of power as a first step toward a more just society" (Delpit, 1988, p. 280; see also Delpit, 2006a, 2006b). As current practitioners, classroom teachers as associated teacher educators are uniquely positioned to engage alongside the preservice and practicing teachers they support to cultivate learning environments which emphasize social justice and make learning accessible to all students.

Among others, actions taken by classroom teachers as associated teacher educators which evidence strong command of Standard 2 include: engagement in culturally responsive pedagogy; demonstration of ways to connect to students' families, cultures, and communities; development and use of assessments that connect content understandings to students' lives and interests; and, demonstration of engagement in activities that promote social justice.

Standard 3—Scholarship. *Engage in inquiry and contribute to scholarship that expands the knowledge base related to teacher education.* Classroom teachers tend to see themselves more as practitioners than researchers and thus seldom connect to academic scholarship aspects of teacher preparation. Examination of practice, however, is essential to effective teaching. "Teachers having a stance of inquiry continually reflect on their past teaching, ask themselves questions to problematize their current practices, and collect and analyze data to inform future pedagogical decisions and teaching practices" (Smith & Heaton, 2013, p. 148).

Gningue, Schroder, and Peach (2014) emphasize the importance of conditions for classroom action research as influences upon the extent to which teachers improve their pedagogical skills, increase construction of explanations understandable to their students, and the thinking and reasoning that undergirds student work products. Collaboration with collegial peers around theme-oriented investigations leads to more frequent, more focused, and richer reflective research by teachers (Gningue et al., 2014).

Research which focuses on student learning in connection with teacher and teacher educator practice is much needed to systematically improve conditions for learners in today's rapidly changing educational contexts. Layered research which explores the roles of teacher educators in supporting research by teachers and teacher candidates leads to improved practice across roles (Gningue et al., 2014).

Classroom teachers as associated teacher educators share authentic concerns regarding student learning with preservice and practicing teachers and are members of shared communities of practice (Lave & Wenger, 1991). Such teacher educators are uniquely positioned to effectively blend theory and practice and to simultaneously affect positive learning outcomes for preservice and practicing teacher and the students they serve.

Among others, actions taken by classroom teachers as associated teacher educators which evidence strong command of Standard 3 include: investigation of theoretical and practical problems, in teaching, learning, and/or teacher education; connecting new knowledge to existing contexts and perspectives; engagement in research and development projects; application of research to teaching practice and/or program or curriculum development; and, dissemination of research findings to the broader teacher education community.

Standard 4—Professional Development. *Inquire systematically into, reflect on, and improve their practice and demonstrate commitment to continuous professional development.* Classroom teachers are well aware of a wide variety of professional development offerings aimed at their role as a classroom teacher. The intent of this standard is to guide the associated teacher educator to engage in professional development as a teacher educator.

As live and vicarious that serve to impact performance accomplishments and offer feedback, classroom teachers are uniquely positioned to positively impact the self-efficacy beliefs of preservice and practicing teachers (Bandura, 1977). Engagement in collaborative reflection, learner-centered research (Gningue et al., 2014), and demonstration and application of understandings of differences between feedback, advice, and evaluation (Wiggins, 2012) assist classroom teachers in advancing their own and others' pedagogical practice.

Active participation in professional organizations centered upon teacher education and content/grade-level disciplines helps classroom teachers as associated teacher educators to engage within the community of practice of teacher educators and to gain support in applying their professional understandings to the initial and ongoing learning of teachers (Wenger, McDermott, & Snyder, 2002).

Among others, actions taken by classroom teachers as associated teacher educators which evidence strong command of Standard 4 include: participate in and reflect on learning activities in professional associations and learned societies; apply life experiences to teaching and learning; engage in collaborative reflection, goal setting, and examination of professional practice with other teacher educators; and, engage in observation and analysis of teaching and learning events across instructional settings.

Standard 5—Program Development. *Provide leadership in developing, implementing, and evaluating teacher education programs that are rigorous, relevant, and grounded in theory, research, and best practice.* Classroom teachers as associated teacher educators significantly influence teacher development through classroom modeling. Wilson, Floden, and Ferrini-Mundy assert, "Experienced and newly certified teachers alike see clinical experiences as a powerful—sometimes the single most powerful—element of teacher preparation" (2002, p. ii).

Student teachers adopt the practices and dispositions modeled by partnering teachers (McIntyre, 2009). Classroom teachers as associated teacher educators are uniquely positioned to influence initial and continuing teacher education programs through connections made between campus-based coursework and the actual experience of teaching. Classroom teachers have been identified as the "best placed people to model classroom teaching, to plan the student teachers' practice of classroom teaching and to give feedback on the students' classroom teaching" (McIntyre, 2009, p. 602).

In 1995, the Holmes Group recommended the development of clinical professorships as an avenue for distinguished school practitioners to collaborate with university faculty to make significant contributions to programs of teaching and inquiry (Holmes Group, 1995). However, teacher education programs rarely leverage the rich opportunity to utilize the classroom-based teacher educators' expertise in the development, implementation, and evaluation of teacher education programs.

Many classroom teachers prioritize attention to the welfare of their classroom students due to lack of coordination of their responsibilities, time, and training across the school and university contexts (McIntyre, 2009). In addition to field-based roles, classroom teachers often engage in campus-based teacher education as adjunct faculty.

The Professional Development School partnership model has demonstrated success in linking school and university teacher educators (Darling-Hammond, 2006). In this capacity, as well, potential contributions to program development are embraced. Deepened collaboration and heightened valuation of diverse forms of expertise support maximized the utilization of the expertise of classroom teachers as associated teacher educators (Zeichner, Payne, & Brayko, 2015).

Among others, actions taken by classroom teachers as associated teacher educators which evidence strong command of Standard 5 include: lead or actively contribute to the ongoing assessment of teacher education courses or programs; contribute to research that focuses on effective teacher education programs; and, participate actively in the alignment of courses and/or programs to reflect theory, research, and best practice.

Standard 6—Collaboration. *Collaborate regularly and in significant ways with relevant stakeholders to improve teaching, research, and student learning.* Classroom teachers interact with multiple stakeholders to inform teaching practice and to yield networks and resources which improve teaching, research, and student learning. Such stakeholders include universities, schools, families, communities, foundations, businesses, and museums, among others.

Hybrid spaces, "where academic, practitioner, and community-based knowledge come together in new ways to support the development of innovative and hybrid solutions to the problem of preparing teachers," have recently been proposed as an improvement upon traditional and early entry forms of teacher preparation (Zeichner et al., 2015, p. 124). Classroom teachers as associated teacher educators are uniquely positioned as boundary spanners who can cultivate relationships with diverse stakeholders to support the achievement of goals rooted in understandings of students and their learning needs.

Day argues that "much research about teachers and teaching is still planned and conducted by researchers who give little thought or effort to the involvement and learning of the teachers who are their subjects" (1991, p. 537). Collaborations in research between classroom teachers as associated teacher educators, their campus-based counterparts, and family and community stakeholders hold promise to initiate and expand communities of practice. Collaborative research and support for teacher learning expands the perspectives that contribute to teacher knowledge and responsiveness to the changing student populations they serve (Zeichner et al., 2015).

Among others, actions taken by classroom teachers as associated teacher educators which evidence strong command of Standard 6 include: engagement in cross-institutional and cross-college partnerships; participation in joint decision making about teacher education; initiation of collaborative projects that contribute to improved teacher education; and, fostering of cross disciplinary endeavors.

Standard 7—Public Advocacy. *Serve as informed, constructive advocates for high-quality education for all students.* Public advocacy occurs at several levels at which classroom teachers as associated teacher educators are particularly equipped to contribute to the improvement of education for all learners. At the classroom, school, and district levels, accomplished classroom teachers model the development of democratic classroom structures and advocacy for individuals and groups of learners.

As lifelong learners, these classroom teachers stay informed of issues which impact education and engage in critical investigation of reform movements, considering how recommendations and courses of action impact students in light of rapidly changing needs. Whereas "public advocacy efforts, generally, are not embedded components in teacher education coursework" (Venditti, 2009, p. 102), classroom teachers have the capacity to engage the preservice and practicing teachers they work with in classroom-based projects, research initiatives, and community engagement activities which demonstrate and unpack advocacy within authentic educational and political contexts (Ladson-Billings, 1995).

Classroom teachers as associated teacher educators interact with educator preparation programs and have important understandings of the challenges and potential solutions emergent in the processes of creating and sustaining high-quality field-based learning experiences for educators. Through collaboration with campus-based teacher educators and researchers, classroom teachers as associated teacher educators can enact advocacy in professional learning of peers to address concerns.

Beck and Kosnik (2002) found that teacher candidates experience great variation in relationships with cooperating teachers such that some student teachers report receiving little guidance whereas others receive demonstrations and discussion of teaching practices to emulate. Through advocacy directed toward their district and university partners, classroom teachers as associated teacher educators can advocate for much-needed mentorship training (Ganser, 2002) for field-based teacher educators and can conduct research which illuminates what such training should appropriately include.

When asked about using the ATE teacher educator standards in their practice this is the area that provides the most challenge. Needs assessment data have shown that public advocacy is uncomfortable for many teacher educators (Holbert, 2012). Participating teacher educators identified a lack of training or preparation for public advocacy and suggested that the potential for adverse interpretations of/responses to public advocacy efforts inhibited their activities with regard to this standard.

Dinkelman, Margolis, and Sikkenga (2006) found that new campus-based teacher educators had very localized approaches to advocacy and pursued issues of programming and practice which were closely linked to priorities developed during their classroom teaching. Collaborations among primary and associated teacher educators hold promise to leverage advocacy focused specifically on teacher and student learning to contribute to student-centered efforts across organizational contexts.

Among others, actions taken by classroom teachers as associated teacher educators which evidence strong command of Standard 7 include:

- Promoting quality education for all learners through community forums, activities with other professionals, and work with local policy makers;
- Informing and educating those involved in making governmental policies and regulations at local, state, and/or national levels to support and improve teaching and learning; and,
- Actively addressing policy issues which affect the education profession;

Advocating within schools and districts:

- To promote approaches to teaching and learning which maximize simultaneous benefits to learners across P-12 and teacher education programs; and,
- Modeling and promoting reflection teaching and learning strategies which prompt teachers and P-12 learners to challenge social and political perceptions, policies, and systems which limit access to high-quality educational experiences for all learners.

Standard 8—Teacher Education Profession. *Contribute to improving the teacher education profession.* Classroom teachers as associated teacher educators are positioned to enhance the teacher education profession through engagement in disciplinary and pedagogical professional organizations, through their capacity to contextualize research to relevant contexts and to contribute to the professional learning of school- and campus-based teacher educators. Active engagement in disciplinary professional associations provides classroom teachers with a wealth of content and pedagogical knowledge.

Application of new knowledge and engagement in action research focused on student learning contextualizes theoretical constructs and illuminates the ways in which they work for individuals and groups in authentic contexts (Daniel & Poole, 2009; Gningue et al., 2014). Collaborative research within the authentic classroom contexts stands to improve the profession by illuminating issues that are often inadequately attended to when educational theories are developed in controlled settings (Daniel & Poole, 2009).

Much research elaborates the disconnect between theory and practice which contributes to teacher reluctance to implement campus-originated educational interventions. For example, Tom (1997) describes his experience as a campus-based staff developer, stating "we teacher educators are too willing to detach theoretical study from teaching practice. I found the high school teachers unwilling to consider theoretical issues about the selection and adaptation of social studies curricula apart from using these curricula with students" (p. 9).

Partnership between classroom teachers as associated teacher educators and campus-based teacher educators offers an impetus for increased teacher motivation as well as multifaceted vantage points to inform the content and delivery of professional education experiences (Zeichner et al., 2015).

Through mentorship and collaboration with school-based colleagues, classroom teachers as associated teacher educators are also uniquely positioned to train and recruit school personnel who may serve as the next generation of school-based and adjunct program faculty. Classroom teachers as associated teacher educators also have significant impacts on teacher candidate learning.

The perception that campus-based teacher educators hold greater influence than classroom teachers on the shape and quality of the profession (Isham, Carter, & Stribling, 1981; Reynolds, McCollough, Bendixen-Noe, & Morrow, 1994) is highly contested by evidence of cooperating teacher impacts on teacher candidates. Anderson (2007) found that student teachers most commonly cite their cooperating teachers as having had an impact on their changes. Personal experiences emergent within the culture of teaching also strongly influence the decision making and critical reflection of teachers (Sim, 2011).

Guyton and McIntyre (1990) cited negative socializing pressures of school sites as a key shortcoming of teacher programs. Leveraging the expertise and contributions of classroom teacher who focus on teacher education roles as associated teacher educators offers one solution to this long-standing challenge.

Among others, actions taken by classroom teachers as associated teacher educators which evidence strong command of Standard 8 include: recruiting promising preservice teachers; recruiting future teacher educators; supporting student organizations to advance teacher education; mentoring colleagues toward professional excellence; actively participating in professional organizations at the local, state, national, or international levels; and, writing/editing/reviewing manuscripts for publication or presentation for teacher education organizations.

Standard 9—Vision. *Contribute to creating visions for teaching, learning, and teacher education that take into account such issues as technology, systemic thinking, and worldviews.* Through the decades of teacher preparation and inservice staff development, classroom teachers have often been critical of the training and other professional development they received. There are now opportunities for teachers to have a voice in creating better programming at all levels by speaking up and recommending alternative programming.

Classroom teachers as associated teacher educators should be valued for the linkages they identify and convey to preservice and practicing teachers regarding the changing context of classrooms and the history, current events, and future priorities of education in a rapidly globalizing society. Classroom teachers have the capacity to create learning experiences for students in which they actively examine impacts of a wide variety of social issues and take action to create positive changes within their neighborhoods and communities.

Through collaborative design and systematic inquiries into empowering learning experiences, classroom teachers as associated teacher educators can broaden other educators' understandings of how to make positive impacts on schools and communities through their teaching. As learner populations become increasingly diverse, classroom teachers are called upon to understand the realities of students' communities and social positions and conditions to "attempt to raise the students' identity, provide equitable access to appropriate curriculum and instruction and remedy any existing harmful inequities" (Lalas, 2007, p. 17).

Through mentorship and school-based professional learning, classroom teachers as associated teacher educators can help preservice and practicing teachers to recognize and respond to intersections of global, societal, and demographic factors which impact student learning. In combination, the enactment of multiple standards including cultural competence, collaboration, and professional development and scholarship assists classroom teachers as associated teacher educators in making decisions which impact the education contexts and teaching capacity available to future generations.

The developments of visions for teaching and teacher education hinge upon the ongoing dynamic interaction of the learner, the teacher, and the classroom context. Specifically, Lalas (2007) appropriately identifies the intersection of personal, and research-based, and global knowledge in the construction of meaning, stating "both the learner and the teacher use their life experiences, personal values and beliefs, personal and world knowledge, abilities to construct, monitor, and represent knowledge, and personal meaning construction and decision-making disposition in the instructional context of the classroom" (p. 20).

Each of the previous standards provides ways to implement ideas, but this standard urges all teacher educators to look "outside of the box" to see better alternatives. Among others, actions taken by classroom teachers as associated teacher educators which evidence strong command of Standard 9 include: promoting innovation adoption with research; relating new knowledge about global issues to own practice and P-12 classroom teaching; articulating innovation in the field of teacher education; and, actively participating in learning communities that focus on educational change.

Each standard and its role is paralleled to role-related capacities and applications for the Classroom Teacher as an Associated Teacher Educator in the following table.

**ASSOCIATED TEACHER EDUCATORS
USING STANDARDS FOR TEACHER EDUCATORS**

Teacher Educator Standard	Indicators Excerpted from Standards On Line See Standards for Additional Indicators
STANDARD 1	• Model effective instruction to meet the needs of diverse learners • Demonstrate and promote critical thinking and problem solving among teacher educators, teachers, and/or prospective teachers • Model reflective practice to foster student reflection • Mentor novice teachers and/or teacher educators • Facilitate professional development experiences related to effective teaching practices
STANDARD 2	• Professionally participate in diverse communities • Model ways to reduce prejudice for preservice and in-service teachers and/or other educational professionals • Demonstrate connecting instruction to students' families, cultures, and communities • Promote inquiry into cultures and differences • Teach a variety of assessment tools that meet the needs of diverse learners • Recruit diverse teachers and teacher educators
STANDARD 3	• Apply research to teaching practice and/or program or curriculum development • Participate in program evaluation • Engage in action research • Systematically assess learning goals and outcomes
STANDARD 4	• Systematically reflect on own practice and learning • Engage in purposeful professional development focused on professional learning goals • Develop and maintain a philosophy of teaching and learning that is continuously reviewed based on a deepening understanding of research and practice • Participate in and reflect on learning activities in professional associations and learned societies
STANDARD 5	• Lead or actively contribute to the ongoing assessment of teacher education courses or programs • Contribute to research that focuses on effective teacher education programs

(continued)

Teacher Educator Standard	**Indicators** *Excerpted from Standards On Line* *See Standards for Additional Indicators*
STANDARD 6	• Engage in cross-institutional and cross-college partnerships • Participate in joint decision making about teacher education • Initiate collaborative projects that contribute to improved teacher education
STANDARD 7	• Promote quality education for all learners through community forums, activities with other professionals, and work with local policy makers • Actively address policy issues which affect the education profession
STANDARD 8	• Actively participate in professional organizations at the local, state, national, or international level • Recruit promising preservice teachers • Recruit future teacher educators • Support student organizations to advance teacher education
STANDARD 9	• Actively participate in learning communities that focus on educational change • Demonstrate innovation in the field of teacher education • Demonstrate qualities of an early adopter of technology and new configurations of learning

Additional indicators of each of these roles are provided in the full standards document available on the ATE website (ATE, 2003). Taken together, understanding and enactment of these roles supports classroom teachers to increase the quality of preservice and in-service teacher education. These standards exist as statements of guidance which identify ways for the classroom teacher to grow professionally to make an impact on the education of teachers.

Classroom teachers are often overlooked in terms of their pivotal contributions to teacher development. In the section that follows, two classifications of teacher educators, primary teacher educators and associated teacher educators, are elaborated to clarify the nature of these teacher educators' work.

TEACHER EDUCATOR IDENTITIES—DEFINING AND REDEFINING WHO COUNTS AS A TEACHER EDUCATOR

Those who teach, supervise, or mentor in programs designed to result in teacher credentialing or continued professional growth, no matter who employs them, are appropriately identified as teacher educators and serve as the primary influence on future teachers in educator preparation programs. In traditional teacher education programs, the term *teacher educator* has typically been used to refer to university faculty (Ducharme, 1986; Fisher, 2009).

However, over time, conceptualizations of teacher educators have broadened in recognition of additional stakeholder groups who enact teacher educator roles resulting in substantial impacts on the initial and ongoing development of educators. "The concept of who is a teacher educator is not widely accepted, is under continual rethinking, and is impacted by changes in teacher education programs" (Fisher, 2009, p. 29). The Standards for Teacher Educators are an operational definition of the activities of teacher educators and can be used to guide associated selection and continued professional learning aims.

Teacher educator identities are not defined by institutions, positions, or titles, but rather by how individuals approach their work, are prepared, and influence teacher development (Fisher, 2009). Teacher educators may include personnel from higher education institutions, schools, and other entities which design, implement, and evaluate teachers' professional learning.

Across program types, limited coordination between course and field components of teacher education is often cited as an important shortcoming (Anderson & Stillman, 2011; Zeichner, 2010). Classroom teachers as associated teacher educators, however, hold unique potential to support upon coordination efforts. Classroom teachers are a consistent factor as mentors and supports to candidate learning about effective teaching (Anderson, 2007). Recognition and support for the work of classroom teachers as associated teacher educators is an important starting point to address identified challenges.

To address the challenges of developing linkages between campus and field-based learning, some programs have moved methods courses to schools settings and have involved P-12 teachers in the instruction of teacher candidates (e.g., Jeffery & Polleck, 2013; Klein, Taylor, Onore, Strom, & Abrams, 2013; Morgan-Fleming, Simpson, Curtis, & Hull, 2010; Shirley et al., 2006). Though such actions represent early efforts toward collaboration and potential exchange of expertise, classroom teachers' work is often undervalued.

The "hidden curriculum of existing models of teacher education (Ginsburg & Clift, 1990) often sends a very clear message about the lack of respect for the knowledge of P-12 practitioners and non-professional educators in communities" (Zeichner et al., 2015, p. 124). Zeichner et al. (2015) assert,

> Simply moving a methods course to a school and involving P-12 teachers in the instruction of teacher candidates does not necessarily mean that the teachers' expertise is valued and utilized in the ways that we advocate; attention to the democratic qualities of collaboration is necessary. . . . In the examples that best denote horizontal expertise, classroom teachers are active participants in the planning, instruction, and evaluation activities related to a course, thereby

creating more authentic, acceptable an accessible possibilities for inclusion of teachers' expertise. (p. 127)

Darling-Hammond (2006) quotes teachers to offer an exemplar of the valuation of the expertise of classroom teachers as associated teacher educators. These teachers' experiences help to illuminate how an understanding of the capacities of classroom teachers as associated teacher educators motivates teachers while putting their professional knowledge to maximized use in preparation of the next generation of professionals:

> The university faculty treated us like professionals. They asked *us* what *we* needed to do for our campus. They wanted to know what *we* thought . . . it was one of the first times someone had asked our opinion. [They] challenged us, supported us, and made us feel that yes, we can do something. We can break the cycle, we can make a difference, it was a wonderful feeling to be trusted and respected and to have someone believe in us. Their support and encouragement empowered us to know that we could come up with a solution.
>
> Just as it was a shot in the arm when they asked us what we wanted to do for Hawthorne, we were honored when Dr. Moore [director of Trinity's teacher education program] asked us to help Trinity create a fifth-year teacher education program. They wanted to know what we saw as the critical pieces necessary for becoming a master teacher. Trinity faculty asked Hawthorne teachers what ingredients were needed to ensure a teacher a successful start and therefore a successful future. (p. 178)

Examples of successful interactions of classroom teachers as associated teacher educators and campus-based teacher educators should be used as models and starting points to fuel ongoing improvements within the field of teacher education.

INTERSECTIONS OF STANDARDS IN THE ROLES OF CLASSROOM TEACHERS AS ASSOCIATED TEACHER EDUCATORS

Actions of associated teacher educators typically cut across specific aspects of the standards. In this section we will describe some actions that incorporate multiple standards and can be implemented by classroom teachers as associated teacher educators to improve teacher education programs.

- Respond positively when asked to be involved in teacher education roles such as hosting an observer, a methods course student, or a student teacher. Every teacher can justify rejecting such an offer because of the needs of

classroom students or the busy life of the teacher, but accepting the offer can be seen as a professional responsibility.
- Offer to be a mentor to a beginning teacher.
- Participate in professional organizations, such as ATE, that have an agenda for the implementation and improvement of teacher education.
- When participating in ways to improve classroom learning of your students, consider ways to help existing teachers to develop the knowledge, skills, and dispositions needed to implement the ideas.
- When teacher education and professional development ideas are being considered by your colleagues, be the voice that advocates for serious consideration of solutions to the issues.
- Promote the development of partnerships between your school and an educator preparation program. The benefits of such partnerships can impact your own classrooms.

APPLICATION OF THE STANDARDS

The Standards for Teacher Educators have been used in different ways to provide an operational definition of the work of teacher educators. The following provide brief descriptions of these ways. The Association of Teacher Educators' annual meetings and summer conferences are organized along the standards to promote teacher educators' focus on areas of expertise and to facilitate recognition of areas for new learning through attendance at conference presentations. Examinations of presentations at these meetings highlight the large variety of uses of the standards.

The program for the latest ATE conference, available on the ATE website, can provide a menu of such activity. One of the consistent presentation topics at these meetings demonstrates how the standards have been used as a tool for professional reflection and improvement of practice by individuals and groups of stakeholders in teacher education. Some higher education institutions have used the standards as a component of the annual faculty evaluation process. The standards provide a reference point for describing the work of faculty engaged in teacher education, distinguishing their work from other higher education faculty. The standards also inform research by teacher educators within and beyond the Association of Teacher Educators.

CONCLUSIONS

This is an exciting time for program development in preservice and in-service teacher education. Teacher education partnerships between schools and universities and between schools and staff development providers can benefit from the integration of classroom teachers into active roles in the programs. In this chapter, we sought to identify the varied roles of classroom teachers as associated teacher educators and to introduce the standards as an operational definition of this work.

Classroom teachers as associated teacher educators hold powerful potential with regard to demonstration, rationale building, and clarification of teaching roles. Building on classroom teachers' knowledge of self and students, families, communities and instructional outcomes can support the relevance, equity, and access of learning experiences for both developing educators and the students they serve. Through engagement in professional development focused on their teacher education roles, classroom teachers can elevate the voice of school-based faculty in the conversation around how teachers are best prepared to meet the realities of today's classroom contexts.

Classroom teacher engagement in teacher preparation through program design and provision of feedback supports theory to practice connections and relevance of what beginning and developing teachers learn about educating today's students in ways that motivate and challenge them. These and other collaborations which meld multiple teacher educator roles contribute the expansion of communities of practice to leverage the expertise of educators at all levels.

Working together across boundaries helps classroom teachers as associated teacher educators, along with their campus-based counterparts, to develop and prompt awareness of issues impacting education and to advocate for mutually beneficial solutions. As teacher education moves to a more collaborative stance which embraces the work of teacher educators across organizational boundaries, new approaches to recruitment of teachers and teacher educators become possible.

In addition, collaboration across organizational boundaries among teacher educators serves to foster innovation and attention to the changing needs and priorities of P-12 students and the teachers who engage in ongoing learning to best serve their needs. Consideration of how the Standards for Teacher Educators apply to classroom teachers as associated educators prompts professional roles for teachers that have been long discussed but not yet realized. The future of teacher education rests on the active involvement of all personnel of the education-related institutions.

Future research should include studies of the roles, responsibilities, and role-related capacities of classroom teachers as associated teacher educators. Such studies will provide insights into how collaborative efforts across organizational boundaries support teacher development and student learning. Exploration-layered efforts to simultaneously improve teacher development and P-12 student learning are needed. Such studies hold promise to support boundary spanning in support of improved practice and ongoing responsiveness to the changing needs of learners across demographic categories.

Potential research questions include the following:

- In what ways do preservice and practicing teachers' beliefs about their students' families and communities change through engaged research alongside classroom teachers as associated teacher educators?
- What do campus-based primary teacher educators learn by working alongside classroom teachers as associated teacher educators to address opportunity gaps existing within school and classroom contexts?
- In what ways do pedagogical practices change through the implementation of triadic scholarship efforts between classroom teachers as associated teacher educators, campus-based teacher educators, and teacher candidates?
- What insights into program improvement, recruitment, and retention come from collaborations with classroom teachers as associated teacher educators?
- How can leveraging the knowledge of classroom teachers contribute to the development of pipelines to recruit and retain diverse teacher candidates?
- What forms of community knowledge do classroom teachers utilize to enhance the relevance of student learning?
- How are these forms of knowledge leveraged by teacher candidates working under the collaborative guidance of associated and primary teacher educators?

REFERENCES

Anderson, D. (2007). The role of cooperating teachers' power in student teaching. *Education, 128*(2), 307–323.

Anderson, L., & Stillman, J. (2011). Student teaching for a specialized view of professional practice? Opportunities to learn in and for urban, high-needs schools. *Journal of Teacher Education, 62*(5), 446–464.

Association of Teacher Educators. (2003). Standards for Teacher Educators. Retrieved from http://ate1.org/pubs/Standards.cfm

Aoki, T. T. (1993). Legitimating lived curriculum: Towards a curricular landscape of multiplicity. *Journal of Curriculum and Supervision, 8*(3), 255–268.

Bandura, A. (1977). Self-efficacy: Toward a unifying theory of behavioral change. *Psychological Review, 84*(2), 191–215.

Beck, C., & Kosnik, C. (2002). Components of a good practicum placement: Student teacher perceptions. *Teacher Education Quarterly, 29*(2), 81–98.

Bransford, J. D., Brown, A., & Cocking, R. (Eds.). (2000). *How people learn: Mind, brain, experience and school: Expanded edition*. Washington, DC: National Academy Press.

Clift, R. T. (2009). Be careful of what you ask for: Do we really want or need standards for teacher educators? In C. L. Klecka, S. J. Odell, W. R. Houston, & R. H. McBee (Eds.), *Visions for teacher educators: Perspectives on the Association of Teacher Educators' standards* (pp. 299–313). New York, NY: Rowman & Littlefield.

Cornelius-White, J. D. (2007). Learner-centered teacher-student relationships are effective: A meta-analysis. *Review of Educational Research, 77,* 113–143.

Daniel, D. B., & Poole, D. A. (2009). Learning for life: An ecological approach to pedagogical research. *Perspectives on Psychological Science, 4*(1), 91–96.

Darling-Hammond, L. (2006). *Powerful teacher education: Lessons from exemplary programs.* San Francisco, CA: Jossey-Bass.

Day, C. (1991). Roles and relationships in qualitative research on teachers' thinking: A reconsideration. *Teaching and Teacher Education, 7*(5), 537–547.

Delpit, L. (1988). The silenced dialogue: Power and pedagogy in educating other people's children. *Harvard Educational Review, 58*(3), 280–298.

Delpit, L. (2006a). Educators as "seed people" growing a new future. *Educational Researcher, 7*(32), 14–21.

Delpit, L. (2006b). Lessons from teachers. *Journal of Teacher Education, 57*(3), 220–231.

Dinkelman, T., Margolis, J., & Sikkenga, K. (2006). From teacher to teacher educator: Experiences, expectations, and expatriation. *Studying Teacher Education, 2*(1), 5–23.

Ducharme, E. R. (1986). *Teacher educators: What do we know?* ERIC Digest 15. ED279643. Washington, DC: ERIC Clearinghouse on Teacher Education.

Fisher, R. L. (2009). Who is a teacher educator? In C. L. Klecka, S. J. Odell, W. R. Houston, & R. H. McBee (Eds.), *Visions for teacher educators* (pp. 29–44). New York, NY: Rowman & Littlefield.

Ganser, T. (2002). How teachers compare the roles of cooperating teacher and mentor. *The Educational Forum, 66,* 380–385.

Ginsburg, M., & Clift, R. (1990). The hidden curriculum of preservice teacher education. In W. R. Houston (Ed.), *Handbook of research on teacher education* (pp. 450–468). New York, NY: Macmillan.

Gningue, S. M., Schroder, B., & Peach, R. (2014). Reshaping the "Glass Slipper": The development of reflective practice by mathematics teachers through action research. *American Secondary Education, 42*(3), 18–29.

Graham, B. (2006). Conditions for successful field experiences: Perceptions of cooperating teachers. *Teaching and Teacher Education, 22*(8), 1118–1129.

Guyton, E., & McIntyre, D. (1990). Student teaching and school experiences. In W. Houston (Ed.) *Handbook of research on teacher education* (pp. 514–534). New York, NY: McMillan.

Holbert, R. M. (2012, August). *Standards for teacher educators: A needs assessment of teacher education faculty.* Presented at the Association of Teacher Educators Summer Conference, Cambridge, MA.

Holmes Group. (1995). *Tomorrow's schools of education: A report from the Holmes Group.* East Lansing, MI: Author.

Houston, W. R., Haberman, M., & Silula, J. (Eds.). (1990). *Handbook of research on teacher education*. New York, NY: Macmillan.

Isham, M. M., Carter, H. L., & Stribling, R. (1981). *A study of the entry mechanisms of university-based teacher educators*. Research and Development Center for Teacher Education, University of Texas at Austin. (ERIC Document Reproduction Service No. 230–493).

Jeffery, J. V., & Polleck, J. (2013). Transformations in site-based teacher preparation courses: The benefits and challenges. In J. Noel (Ed.), *Moving teacher education into urban schools and communities* (pp. 105–119). New York, NY: Routledge.

Klein, E., Taylor, M., Onore, C., Strom, K., & Abrams, L. (2013). Finding a third space in teacher education: Creating an urban teacher residency. *Teaching Education, 24*(1), 27–57.

Ladson-Billings, G. (1995). Toward a theory of culturally relevant pedagogy. *American Educational Research Journal, 32*(3), 465–491.

Lalas, J. (2007). Teaching for social justice in multicultural urban schools: Conceptualization and classroom implication. *Multicultural Education, 14*(3), 17–21.

Lave, J., & Wenger, E. (1991). *Situated learning: Legitimate peripheral participation*. New York, NY: Cambridge University Press.

Lawless, K. A., & Pellegrino, J. W. (2007). Professional development in integrating technology into teaching and learning: Knowns, unknowns, and ways to pursue better questions and answers. *Review of Educational Research, 77*(4), 575.

McIntyre, D. (2009). The difficulties of inclusive pedagogy for initial teacher education and some thoughts on the way forward. *Teaching and Teacher Education, 25*(4), 602–608.

Moll, L. C., Amanti, C., Neff, D., & Gonzalez, N. (1992). Funds of knowledge for teaching: Using a qualitative approach to connect homes and classrooms. *Theory into Practice, 31*(2), 132–141.

Morgan-Fleming, B., Simpson, D., Curtis, K., & Hull, W. (2010). Learning through partnership. *Teacher Education Quarterly, 37*(3), 63–80.

Osunde, E. O. (1996). The effect on student teachers of the teaching behaviors of cooperating teachers. *Education, 116*(4), 612–618.

Penuel, W., Fishman, B., Yamaguchi, R., & Gallagher, L. (2007). What makes professional development effective? Strategies that foster curriculum implementation. *American Educational Research Journal, 44*(4), 921–958.

Reynolds, R. J., McCollough, J. D., Bendixen-Noe, M., & Morrow, L. E. (1994). *The need for knowledge about teacher educators*. Unpublished manuscript, Eastern Connecticut State University. (ERIC Document Reproduction Service No. ED 372–041).

Shirley, D., Hersi, A., MacDonald, E., Sanchez, M. T., Scandone, C., Skidmore, C., & Tutwiler, P. (2006). Bringing the community back in: Change, accommodation, and contestation in a school and university partnership. *Equity & Excellence in Education, 39*, 27–36.

Sim, C. (2011). 'You've either got [it] or you haven't'—conflicted supervision of preservice teachers. *Asia-Pacific Journal of Teacher Education, 39*(2), 139–149.

Smith, W. M., & Heaton, R. M., (2013). Learning from practice about improving the quality of mathematics teacher research. *Mathematics Teacher Educator, (1)*2, 148–161.

Tom, A. R. (1997). *Redesigning teacher education.* New York: SUNY Press.

Venditti, K. J. (2009). Standard seven: Public advocacy. In C. L. Klecka, S. J. Odell, W. R. Houston, & R. H. McBee (Eds.), *Visions for teacher educators: Perspectives on the Association of Teacher Educators' standards* (pp. 101–106). New York, NY: Rowman & Littlefield.

Wenger, E., McDermott, R. A., & Snyder, W. (2002). *Cultivating communities of practice: A guide to managing knowledge.* Boston, MA: Harvard Business Press.

Wiggins, G. (2012). Seven keys to effective feedback. *Feedback, 70*(1), 10–16.

Wilson, S. M., Floden, R. E., & Ferrini-Mundy, J. (2002). Teacher preparation research: An insider's view from the outside. *Journal of Teacher Education, 53*(3), 190–204.

Zeichner, K. (2010). Rethinking the connections between campus courses and field experiences in college and university-based teacher education. *Journal of Teacher Education, 89*(11), 89–99.

Zeichner, K., Payne, K. A., & Brayko, K. (2015). Democratizing teacher education. *Journal of Teacher Education, 66*(2), 122–135.

Chapter 2

Context Is Everything

Increasing the Relevance of Preservice Teachers' Experiences in Classroom Management

Benjamin R. Wellenreiter

ABSTRACT

Teacher education programs are often criticized by their graduates for inadequately addressing the topic of classroom management. Graduates describe these experiences as having little relevance to actual school and classroom conditions. Preservice teacher training in classroom management, without experiences in deep analyses of school and classroom contexts, limits the relevance of this important aspect of teacher preparation.

These contexts are influenced, in part, by varying behavioral norms in different school contexts, multiple authority structures within schools, the fluid nature of behavioral norms within contexts, and teacher/student and student/student histories and relationships. Teacher preparation experiences that emphasize analysis and understanding of context encourage flexible, informed, and proactive approaches to classroom management concerns. Activities that encourage deeper contextual understanding are described and implications for teacher education programs are discussed.

KEYWORDS

Classroom management, school discipline, student behavior, teacher education

The prompt discussion seemed simple enough: "Blake's comments were seen as rude by the other members of his group. How would you respond to him or to the group?"

"Well, it depends." Claire, a pre-student teaching education major in a middle school philosophy class, responded. "Has he done this before?"

"From time to time Blake's comments can come across as kind of harsh. So, yes, I suppose he has done this previously." I stated.

"Ok. Well then chances are I have said something to him about this already. He should know better. I would give him a detention for the rudeness." Claire said.

"Would your response to Blake change if you were aware his mother called yesterday to let you know that some of the group members were teasing him in the cafeteria?" I asked.

Claire considered carefully, then said; "It might. I would want to know more about that."

"Why would it matter?" I prod, "Your classroom rules clearly state students are to respect one another and that infractions of this rule can lead to detention."

"But it is not as clear cut as that. If something that is happening outside the classroom is affecting his behavior, it should be taken into consideration. I don't want to make him a victim twice."

"Would you change your approach if you knew one of the students teasing Blake was also his step-brother who was currently living with Blake's father?" I add.

"Oh boy . . ." Claire responds.

Throughout the conversation details emerged that informed and ultimately worked to help Claire respond to this prompt. She gradually came to the conclusion that she would need to have a relationship with the students involved to come to a fair, informed response. For the sake of the hypothetical situation, we concluded that a detention and a phone call to Blake's mother was the best course of action.

In reality, this approach could have done more harm than good. In this scenario, as with all issues that arise in schools and their classrooms, current context and history play vital roles in the application of appropriate classroom management strategies and actions. By focusing attention on contextual factors that influence student behavior, teachers can work to make their responses to issues more flexible and appropriate to the situation.

As both a middle-school teacher and adjunct faculty member at a nearby university, I have the opportunity to bring recent, detailed scenarios from my middle-school environment to preservice teachers to analyze and discuss. Simple behavioral observations and requests for how teachers should respond evolve into discussions that evoke consideration of context, culture, socioeconomic status, authority structures, and student–teacher relationships.

Going well beyond creating a list of classroom rules and procedures, the teacher preparation classes of which I am a part work to understand how context and deep relationships with students are important informants of appropriate classroom management approaches.

The teacher education candidates with whom I work describe these scenario discussions as being immensely helpful experiences in informing their future classroom management approaches. These scenarios, in addition to teacher candidate observations in school settings beyond the classroom, discussions of different levels of authority systems, discussions of the fluid nature of contextual norms, and emphasis on relationships over procedures, may encourage more nuanced and flexible consideration of classroom management processes.

Much of this chapter works to broaden the generally understood conceptualization of classroom management to include extra-classroom contexts and student histories. Because of this, it is important to detail what is meant by the term *classroom management*. Jackson, Simoncini, and Davidson (2013) argue for a nuanced application of the term:

> Our choice of the term classroom management rather than the often used behaviour management is indicative of our belief that the teachers' professional reflections should holistically focus on the classroom environment inclusive of teacher strategies and student behavior rather than solely focus on student (mis) behavior. (p. 30–31)

Taking this approach further, the current chapter works to widen the scope of teacher/student interaction to include extra-classroom settings—where much behavior occurs. Though the term *classroom management* limits this view, it is appreciated that it is a ubiquitous term and is not likely to be extinguished in lieu of a broader label. Throughout the chapter, *classroom management* is defined as the strategies and actions, both proactive and reactive, the teacher employs when interacting with students in all school settings, classrooms and elsewhere.

This chapter begins by describing criticisms of classroom management experiences in teacher education programs. It then discusses the importance of emphasizing context with preservice teachers when discussing classroom management. The chapter concludes with suggestions for activities that can work to increase the relevance of classroom management experiences for preservice teachers.

CRITICISMS OF CLASSROOM MANAGEMENT EXPERIENCES IN TEACHER EDUCATION PROGRAMS

Lack of Preparation

Knowledge and appropriate application of classroom management strategies are widely accepted as prerequisites for safe and educationally sound classroom environments. Teachers, however, report having few experiences in their preparation programs that adequately address this basic area of professional practice (Ficarra & Quinn, 2014). Perhaps as a result, teachers feel they need more preparation in the areas of classroom management and teacher/student interaction (Chesley & Jordan, 2012; Ergül, Baydik, & Demir, 2013; Friedman, 2000; Johansen, Little, & Akin-Little, 2011; Monroe, Blackwell, & Pepper, 2010).

Going beyond self-reporting, observations of teachers in the field also point to a lack of skill in management of the classroom (Akhtar & Akbar, 2011). The implications of inadequate classroom management preparation can be deep and long-lasting. Lack of classroom management skill can lead to issues ranging from decreased academic achievement to higher rates of teacher burnout (Aloe, Amo, & Shanahan, 2014; Freiberg, Huzinec, & Templeton, 2009).

It is clear that adequate preparation in classroom management is essential and that teachers feel they have not received enough of it in their teacher education preparation programs. Perhaps contributing to this perception is the broadening scope of requirements that must be included in teacher education program plans of study. Top-down, mandated content required of teacher education programs is problematic for teacher educators as they seek to include increased content into finite programs of study (Aronson & Anderson, 2013).

With an increasing number of mandates regarding the content of teacher education programs, teacher educators feel pressure to increase both the depth and breadth of experiences. Unfortunately, this pressure may create the opposite effect by encouraging teacher educators to skim over important concepts in lieu of articulated, often academically oriented, topics. The result may be lip service to professional skills that are traditionally in the periphery of teacher preparation programs: relationship building, social justice, professional development, and classroom management, among others.

To support teachers as they engage in multifaceted roles, deep discussions regarding classroom management and the relationships between teachers and students must be organized. Academic excellence, a main goal of educators, can only take place in climates that are framed by informed, caring, and effective classroom management approaches.

GAP BETWEEN TEACHER PREPARATION PROGRAM EXPERIENCES AND SCHOOL/CLASSROOM REALITIES

Layered upon the concern that there is too little preparation in the area of classroom management is a perceived gap between what teachers learn in their education preparation and what they experience in the field (Chelsey & Jordan, 2012; Dicke, Elling, Schmeck, & Leutner, 2015; Eisenman, Edwards, & Cushman, 2015; Friedman, 2000; Garland, Garland, & Vasquez III, 2013). This gap, often described as a lack of relevance to classroom settings, suggests that the classroom management experiences preservice teachers do receive are inadequate in their content (Chelsey & Jordan, 2012; Eisenman et al., 2015).

Not only are the classroom management experiences infrequent, but they are also viewed as not relevant enough to adequately apply in classroom settings "in the field".

A more specific criticism described by new teachers is a perceived lack of credibility of professors who are not actively working in P-12 settings (Chesley & Jordan, 2012). These teachers describe how workload, collaboration, and contextually specific issues are not adequately addressed in teacher preparation programs: "Respondents reported that coursework having to do with student management and establishing classroom routines was of little value when they were confronted with *real* [emphasis added] students" (ibid, p. 42).

The framing of the concern around the "real" student and the "real" classroom points to a desire for deeper investigation of the context in which the teacher/student relationship occurs. Reflecting this desire, preservice teachers report that they find "greater satisfaction with experiential training sources, (e.g., mentoring from teachers, supervised fieldwork) than academic training sources (e.g., mentoring by professors, stand-alone classroom management sources)" (Christofferson & Sullivan, 2015, p. 258).

Indeed, a large part of the ivory tower criticism with respect to teacher educators is the lack of knowledge of the intricacies of any given educational context. The authority structures, codified and tacit rules, individual personalities, and group dynamics with which teachers daily interact are not adequately addressed in many teacher education classes. To counter this criticism, an increasing focus on discussions of, and experience in, contexts in which classroom management and teaching in general occurs may work to bridge the gap between what takes place in the teacher preparation classroom and the K-12 classroom.

The Association of Teacher Educators (2008) addresses the program/classroom context gap in its standards, charging teacher educators to employ approaches that encourage cultural competence in diverse school settings. Indicators of Standard 2, which addresses cultural competence, include: exhibiting practices that enhance the understanding of diversity, demonstrating the ability to connect instruction to students' cultures and communities, fostering a positive regard for students' backgrounds, and promoting inquiries into culture and differences (Association of Teacher Educators, 2008).

Put into practice, these indicators can be seen in teacher preparation courses when deep, directed discussions about the factors that influence student behavior take place. As teacher educators should understand the cultural contexts of preservice teachers, so too should preservice teachers work to understand the cultural contexts of their students.

Certainly, teacher educators cannot know the specific responsibilities, cultural norms, and histories of all school settings in which preservice and certified teachers work. Within teacher education programs, the goal is not to address every specific concern into which a preservice teacher may run, but to provide them with experiences in asking more meaningful questions about context and history before engaging in classroom management planning and action.

IMPORTANCE OF CONTEXT IN UNDERSTANDING STUDENT BEHAVIOR

The concepts of classroom management, and, more broadly, interpersonal interactions between teachers and students, are vital components of teacher preparation. Though these complicated areas are often conceptualized as rule-making and how to deal with student misbehavior, it is important to widen the scope of this conceptualization to encourage preservice teachers to approach teacher/student interaction more holistically. Schools contain more than classrooms. Additionally, teachers, students, and staff members interact with one another outside of these classrooms.

The authority structures, cultures, and histories of the different spaces in a school, as well as spaces outside of school, influence one another in complex ways that point to a need to view classroom management and teacher/student interactions holistically. Within the classroom, instructional goals, subject matter, and specific student characteristics have an impact on the interaction between teachers and students (Emmer & Stough, 2001).

The same concept holds true to spaces outside the classroom; the purpose of the space and the population of that space have an impact on the behaviors that take place there. To better understand how various settings and interactions therein influence the behaviors and interactions of students, preservice teachers need experience in identification, definition, and analysis of factors that play roles in student behaviors.

Crucial elements in effective classroom management approaches have long been researched (Emmer & Stough, 2001; Kounin & Obradovik, 1967; Simonsen, Fairbanks, Briesch, Myers, & Sugai, 2008). Simonsen et al. (2008) describe:

> [F]ive empirically supported *critical features* of effective classroom management: (a) maximize structure; (b) post, teach, review, monitor, and reinforce expectations; (c) actively engage students in observable ways; (d) use a continuum of strategies for responding to appropriate behaviors and (e) use a continuum of strategies to respond to inappropriate behaviors. (p. 353, italics in original)

Though the elements shown here have been demonstrated to be important, there is less discussion of what information is used to create a classroom management system with these characteristics.

Maximizing structure, for example, without considering the context of the environment, may lead to either overstructured or understructured environments, depending on the situation. Likewise, the creation of a continuum of strategies before understanding the cultures and contexts of student behavior may lead to overly rigid, ineffective, or inappropriate teacher/student interaction. What is needed is discussion of the characteristics of effective classroom management approaches balanced with the factors that inform them.

BEHAVIORAL NORMS AND HISTORIES IN DIFFERENT SCHOOL CONTEXTS

Nested within any school are different contexts in which students behave and interact. School busses, hallways, cafeterias, locker rooms, sports fields, and classrooms are examples of contexts that are rich in authority structures, cultures, and histories that inform student behavior and interaction (Bettis & Adams, 2005; Fingerson, 2005; Heffernan & Lewison, 2005; Jewett, 2005). Physical layout, amount of time spent, and the population of students in different contexts are just a few of the factors that play roles in the complex interaction between students and teachers in these settings (Meyer, Astor, & Behre, 2004).

The appropriateness of an action is informed by the context in which it takes place. Shouting, for example, may be acceptable in certain circumstances (during game-play in physical education) while it may not be acceptable in others (during standardized test-taking). Though this concept may certainly be obvious to preservice teachers, frequent discussion of the contextualization of behaviors may work to encourage more systematic design and implementation of flexible classroom management strategies.

The ubiquitous "respect others" rule that is seen throughout school settings can be interpreted and applied in many ways, depending on local context and history. "Respect others" may be manifested in one way in the cafeteria and in a very different way in the classroom. The teacher who interprets the "respect others" rule in the same way across settings may underestimate the influence the setting has on behavior. Deep discussion of this rule, using multiple contexts as examples, encourages preservice teachers to work into their classroom management more informed questions regarding student behavior.

Discussing how respect is demonstrated in different contexts, combined with questions regarding how interactions in different settings influence one another, reveals the complex interaction of environments and expectations. Discussions of this interaction may encourage a broader understanding of the intricacies of behavioral norms that exist in these places. The result may be teachers who are better prepared to enter, and better respond to, student behavior in these spaces.

In addition to having unique characteristics that inform behavior, different context conditions and histories influence one another. Teachers who recognize and employ this concept may be more adept at classroom management interactions because their views of student behaviors may be more nuanced than those who view student behaviors as being influenced only by the immediate contexts. Conditions that exist and events that occur on playgrounds, in locker rooms, and at lunch influence what happens in classrooms and vice versa.

Students who come to class after having been in overcrowded cafeterias with silent lunches bring with them experiences that influence their behavior in the classroom. The real student described in literature is one who moves through different contexts during the day, bringing to each history that further informs behaviors and interactions. Teachers whose preservice and continuing professional development includes only discussion of academic classroom management are not given sufficient opportunities to analyze these complex settings.

Many teachers are required to supervise cafeterias, recess, hallways, and study halls. The physical layouts and purposes of these spaces are different from one another and require different classroom management approaches. Though it may be assumed teachers will learn norms and strategies "on the fly" in these spaces, it may be deeply beneficial to preservice and novice teachers to have had experiences in discussing these vital, but often ignored, aspects of the teacher's professional responsibilities.

Much of the feeling of unpreparedness for the realities of the K-12 teaching position may lie in the ancillary, but vitally important, teacher/student interactions outside the academic classroom. Preservice teachers who have deep discussions about and observations in diverse settings may be better prepared to view their classroom management systems and applications thereof in more holistic and appropriate ways. The result may be both more informed classroom standards and more flexible and appropriate responses to student behaviors.

DIFFERENT SCHOOL AUTHORITY SYSTEMS

The behaviors in which children engage are influenced by the context in which they happen (Fisher & Spencer, 2015; Stormshak, Bierman, Bruschi, Dodge, & Coie, 1999). Because they have different purposes, conditions, histories, and cultures, different school contexts demand different authority structures, expectations for behaviors, and response to appropriate and inappropriate behaviors. Added to the complexity of the specific characteristics of the contexts in which students interact is the fact that they are being influenced by multiple, simultaneous authority structures (Corsaro, 1992).

Laws, school policies, adult, and student authority structures exist within a layered and interactive system of authority. It is important to recognize the complexity of these multiple sets of rules and authority structures that inform and guide student/teacher interaction if teachers are to better create and apply classroom management systems.

National and state laws guide school policies (e.g., rules regarding suspensions and expulsions due to violent acts). Many schools have autonomy to create another layer of rules that inform teachers and students, (e.g., dress code and homework policies). Subcontexts such as hallways, cafeterias, and classrooms within schools also have explicit and tacit rules that guide behavior. Student peer groups have authority structures that influence behavior. Understanding that these different layers of laws and rules inform one another assists preservice teachers in looking beyond their classrooms when creating management procedures.

Discussions of how these layers interact, and sometimes conflict, work to encourage preservice teachers to consider the multiple layers of authority when executing classroom management plans. Dress code rules and application, for example, may differ between the school and the individual teacher. How should a male teacher approach a female student who is violating the dress code? While the teacher may agree with the school's dress code policy and have the policy stated in his classroom, the context may complicate the application of the dress code within the teacher's classroom.

The teacher is balancing multiple layers of authority and multiple standards of behavior when crafting a response to a dress code violation. Simply putting "adhere to dress code" in a set of rules, without discussing how different authority structures interact with the context, does not provide enough information for the teacher to make informed decisions. Providing preservice teachers with opportunities to consider situations in which different layers of rules conflict with one another encourages them to work through potential issues systematically before the stress of an actual situation.

THE FLUID NATURE OF TEACHER/STUDENT AND STUDENT/STUDENT HISTORIES AND RELATIONSHIPS

Every school context has behavioral norms that change over time. Changing populations, events in the setting, and external factors all play roles in behavioral norms and expectations. Student and teacher emotion, social group membership, and other dynamic factors influence teacher/student interaction (Gest, Madill, Zadzora, Miller, & Rodkin, 2014; Hargreaves, 2000; Pearl, Man-Chi, Van Acker, Farmer, & Rodkin, 2007). The "don't smile before Thanksgiving" concept, though educationally unsound, points toward the understanding that norms within contexts change as the individuals within them change.

As contexts influence one another, so too do histories within contexts influence current behavior and climate. Understanding that classroom and other school settings change in their social structures is important because it encourages adaptive classroom management over reactive classroom management. Additionally, there is a correlation between teachers who are in tune to the dynamics of the social interactions within their classrooms and positive school adjustment of students (Gest et al. 2014). Static rules and procedures need to be balanced with changing group norms and histories; consistency needs to be placed into context.

Discussions of fair versus consistent classroom management practices can reveal to preservice teachers the importance of understanding the fluid nature of classroom dynamics. Student relationships that grow and recede, changing social and academic interests, and the changing lives of students and teachers all influence individuals' behavioral interactions in school settings. These changes demand adjustments to the application of rules and classroom management systems. Late homework policies, for example, can be enforced so consistently that they deny justice to students who experience trauma outside of the classroom.

Students who are consistently late with homework assignments for little legitimate reason, however, may require increasing intervention because the intended outcome of the policy is not meeting its goal. In either case, the static "late homework will not be accepted" rule requires deeper and frequent consideration to meet the ever-changing needs of the student. Fairness changes as time passes, and this concept needs to be balanced with consistency.

Experiences in which they consider factors that demand longitudinal changes of classroom management systems encourage preservice teachers to view these systems as living, dynamic contracts instead of static, rigid procedures.

EXPERIENCES FOR PRESERVICE TEACHERS THAT DEEPEN UNDERSTANDING OF CONTEXT

As teacher education curriculum becomes increasingly filled with mandated, often academically oriented topics, it is important that deep discussions of classroom management do not become lost in the shuffle. Moving beyond predetermined rules without consideration of context, Ullucci (2009) suggests that teachers work to foster relationships and build classroom and school communities.

Discussions of how different contexts, authority systems, and the fluid nature of interactions influence behaviors can broaden teachers' views of student behaviors and encourage more responsive approaches to them. To gain a more holistic understanding of student behaviors and classroom management systems, preservice teachers need experiences in which various school contexts are experienced and analyzed.

OBSERVATIONS IN DIVERSE SCHOOL SETTINGS

A vital element of teacher education programs is observation in K-12 classrooms. Preservice teachers' observations of students and teachers in action and in context work to bridge the perceived gap between theory and practice. These experiences are often used to see psychological and pedagogical concepts in action. Encouraging or requiring preservice teachers to observe in nonclassroom settings such as cafeterias, playgrounds, and school dances presents the opportunity to see how different contexts operate and may broaden their views of the whole school experience.

Teachers are often required to manage these spaces as part of their professional responsibilities. It is only fitting that preservice teachers should have experiences of systematic observation and discussions of these spaces.

After engaging in these various spaces, preservice teachers may bring back to their methods classes observations that can be discussed. Instances of widely variable student behavior, effective and ineffective teacher/student interaction, and questions regarding specific school policies and procedures can lead to fruitful discussions of the intricacies of the teaching profession. Observations of recess disagreement can turn into discussions of whether teachers should prearrange membership in reading groups of students who argued on the playground.

Noticing a student not eating lunch can inform teachers as to potential causes of student inattention while in the classroom. Witnessing teachers appropriately address hallway shoving may lead to questions regarding appropriate and inappropriate teacher/student touch.

Providing preservice teachers opportunity to report to their colleagues their observations of these settings allows for a forum to discuss the multifaceted nature of the school environment. In the process of this reporting, preservice teachers may describe many details of student and teacher life that are important to the school processes, but often skipped over or unobserved in classroom-only observations. More is happening in school than what takes place in the classroom. Preservice teacher observation of the many complex spaces of schools can broaden their understanding of the complex influences on student and teacher behavior and interaction.

CLASSROOM MANAGEMENT VIGNETTES

Preservice teachers need opportunities to analyze specific examples of student and teacher interaction in order to gain experience in applying broader classroom management concepts. The first, and too often last, experience preservice teachers have in classroom management systems before student teaching comes in the form of creating a list of classroom rules and procedures.

Detailed vignettes, such as what is alluded to in this chapter's introduction, can place preservice teachers into hypothetical settings where they can practice, without danger, the rules and procedures they have created for their classroom. Though every detail of a context cannot be introduced, the process of working through a vignette can work to make more real the implications of a preservice teacher's classroom management plan.

Vignettes that describe conflicting authority processes, external factors that complicate classroom management plans, and teacher/student ethical situations are beneficial to experience because they reflect the complexity of school settings. Preservice teachers will struggle with decisions as layers of information and context are poured onto a situation with which they are engaged. Simple rules, such as "raise your hand," are analyzed and put into context as the vignettes grow in their complexity.

The process of placing a classroom management plan next to scenarios in which those plans are put to the test encourages preservice teachers to become more systematic in their classroom management design and application. A criticism of teacher education programs is that they do not sufficiently bridge the gap between theory and the realities of school contexts. Vignettes can, to an extent, bring to practice theories discussed in the safety of teacher education courses.

Encouraging preservice teachers to create their own vignettes, and share them with classmates, deepens the experience by requiring them to articulate many of the details that influence the context and the behaviors therein. The result of vignette creation and analysis is a preservice teacher who has had opportunity to analyze their own classroom management system in a safe, albeit incomplete, setting.

EMPHASIZING RELATIONSHIPS OVER PROCEDURES

Greenberg, Putman, and Walsh (2014) describe rule creation, the establishment of routines, the use of praise, how to address misbehavior, and teacher engagement with students as essential elements in effective classroom management. A key to maximizing the effectiveness of each of these elements is the understanding of the contexts in which they are created and executed. Leaving consideration of culture and history out of the rule and procedure creation process denies the influence these factors have in behaviors. Placing rules and procedures over relationships can trap teachers into making decisions that are inappropriate or ineffective.

Through conversations where they ask questions regarding student history and relationships, preservice teachers can uncover the concept that appropriate responses to student situations are context driven. Balanced with the consistency of established rules is the acknowledgment that particular circumstances may overrule procedure. Professional judgment of the application of rules and procedures in any given circumstance is one aspect of classroom management that requires repeated discussion and practice. Too often are rules and procedures created without discussion of the relationships that inform their applications.

When preservice teachers create classroom management plans and procedures, they may be overly focused on the rules and consequences of violating them. What may often be left out is consideration for the relationships that build and change throughout the school year. Though preservice teachers do not yet know their future students, the creation of isolated rules and procedures without discussion of the contexts in which they may be applied limits the effectiveness of the experience. At the heart of these contexts are the relationships that teachers and students have with one another.

Using students they have come to know through observations, fictitious students that are created for the purpose, or their own personal experiences, preservice teachers can hypothesize how relationships inform the application of policies and procedures. Repeatedly hypothesizing throughout the semester reinforces and deepens the understanding of the multidimensional nature of relationships and classroom management. Preservice teachers move from talking about specific responses to student behaviors toward talking about the variables that might be informing the context and the subsequent behaviors.

Doing this encourages preservice teachers to set aside potential initial responses to student behavior in lieu of discussion of context. From an isolated list of rules at the beginning of a semester, preservice teachers may finish with the same set of rules, but a much deeper understanding of the relationship factors that play vital roles in influencing their applications. The net result may be preservice teachers who see the students in front of them before they see the rules and procedures they have created.

IMPLICATIONS FOR TEACHER EDUCATION PROGRAMS

Expanding experiences of classroom management to include nonacademic spaces, cultures, and histories exposes preservice teachers to a larger, and more accurate, reflection of the teaching profession. Rules and procedures pages that fill many preservice teachers' portfolios can be more effective from the beginning of a teaching career if it is understood that many factors influence their creation and application. Though they may have little actual experience in the contexts in which they will be working, preservice teachers can be more experienced in analyzing the surroundings in which behavior takes place.

Growing teacher preparation courses to include experiences that blend academic and nonacademic strategies can help bridge the gap between the perceived isolated concepts of teacher as instructor and teacher as classroom manager. Classroom management, often viewed as a single and isolated element of teacher preparation, can be threaded throughout a preparation program, strengthening its overall effectiveness.

Encouraging preservice teachers to engage in observations in a variety of settings, discussing observations in depth, and discussing scenarios in which classroom management systems are applied bring together many of the K-12 teacher's roles. The result of such experiences may be new teachers who are better prepared to approach the profession with a deeper appreciation of the complex nature of teacher/student and student/student interaction.

CONCLUSION

Two major complaints preservice and in-service teachers have are they receive little experience in classroom management and the experience they do receive does not adequately address the intricacies of actual K-12 settings. Broadening the understanding of, and experiences in, classroom management can work to counter these criticisms and can improve overall teacher effectiveness.

Seeing students in multiple settings, understanding the complex authority structures in which they behave, and working to better appreciate the contexts in which rules are applied can improve classroom management practices. The result of deeper classroom management experiences can be more effective classroom management procedures, less teacher stress, less early career turnover, better academic environments, and an overall improved school experience for students and teachers.

REFERENCES

Akhtar, T., & Akbar, A. (2011). Views of heads about the discrepancies between skills acquired during teacher training programs and skills required in actual classroom. *International Journal of Academic Research, 3*(2), 632–640.

Aloe, A., Amo, L., & Shanahan, M. (2014). Classroom management self-efficacy and burnout: A multivariate meta-analysis. *Educational Psychology Review, 26*(1), 101–126.

Aronson, B., & Anderson, A. (2013). Critical teacher education and the politics of teacher accreditation: Are we practicing what we preach? *Journal for Critical Education Policy Studies, 11*(3), 244–262.

Association of Teacher Educators. (2008). *Standards for Teacher Educators*. Retrieved from http://www.ate1.org/pubs/uploads/tchredstds0308.pdf.

Bettis, P. J., & Adams, N. G. (2005). Landscapes of girlhood. In P. J. Bettis & N. G. Adams (Eds.), *Geographies of girlhood: Identities in-between* (pp. 1–16). Mahwah, NJ: Lawrence Erlbaum Associates.

Chesley, G. M., & Jordan, J. (2012). What's missing from teacher prep. *Educational Leadership, 69*(8), 41–45.

Christofferson, M., & Sullivan, A. L. (2015). Preservice teachers' classroom management training: A survey of self-reported training experiences, content coverage, and preparedness. *Psychology in the Schools, 52*(3), 248–264.

Corsaro, W. A. (1992). Interpretive reproduction in children's peer cultures. *Social Psychology Quarterly, 55*(2), 160–177.

Dicke, T., Elling, J., Schmeck, A., & Leutner, D. (2015). Reducing reality shock: The effects of classroom management skills training on beginning teachers. *Teaching and Teacher Education, 48*, 1–12.

Eisenman, G., Edwards, S., & Cushman, C. A. (2015). Bringing reality to classroom management in teacher education. *The Professional Educator, 39*(1), 1–12.

Emmer, E. T., & Stough, L.M. (2001). Classroom management: A critical part of educational psychology, with implications for teacher education. *Educational Psychologist, 36*(2), 103–112.

Ergül, C., Baydik, B., & Demir, Ş. (2013). Opinions of in-service and pre-service special education teachers on the competencies of the undergraduate special education programs. *Educational Sciences: Theory & Practice, 13*(1), 518–522.

Ficarra, L., & Quinn, K. (2014). Teachers' facility with evidence-based classroom management practices: An investigation of teachers' preparation programmes and in-service conditions. *Journal of Teacher Education for Sustainability, 16*(2), 71–87.

Fingerson, L. (2005). "Only 4-minute passing periods!" Private and public menstrual identities in schools. In P. J. Bettis & N. G. Adams (Eds.), *Geographies of girlhood: Identities in-between* (pp. 115–135). Mahwah, NJ: Lawrence Erlbaum Associates.

Fisher, L., & Spencer, F. (2015). Children's social behaviour for learning (SBL): Reported and observed social behaviours in contexts of school and home. *Social Psychology of Education, 18*(1), 75–99.

Freiberg, H. J., Huzinec, C. A., & Templeton, S. M., (2009). Classroom management—a pathway to student achievement: A study of fourteen inter-city elementary schools. *Elementary School Journal, 110*(1), 63–80.

Friedman, I. A. (2000). Burnout in teachers: Shattered dreams of impeccable professional performance. *Journal of Clinical Psychology, 56*(5), 595–606.

Garland, D., Garland, K. V., & Vasquez III, E. (2013). Management of classroom behaviors: Perceived readiness of education interns. *Journal of the Scholarship of Teaching and Learning, 13*(1), 133–147.

Gest, S.D., Madill, R.A., Zadzora, K.M., Miller, A.M., & Rodkin, P.C. (2014). Teacher management of elementary classroom social dynamics: Associations with changes in student adjustment. *Journal of Emotional and Behavioral Disorders, 22*(2), 107–118.

Greenberg, J., Putman, H., & Walsh, K. (2014). Training our future teachers: Classroom management, revised. *National Council on Teacher Quality*. (ED 556312).

Hargreaves, A. (2000). Mixed emotions: Teachers' perceptions of their interactions with students. *Teaching and Teacher Education, 16*(8), 811–826.

Heffernan, L., & Lewison, M. T. (2005). What's lunch got to do with it? Critical literacy and the discourse of the lunchroom. *Language Arts, 83*(2), 107–117.

Jackson, C., Simoncini, K., & Davidson, M. (2013). Classroom profiling training: Increasing preservice teachers' confidence and knowledge of classroom management skills. *Australian Journal of Teacher Education, 38*(8), 29–46.

Jewett, L. (2005). Power beads, body glitter, and backseat bad-asses: Girls, power, and position on the school bus. In P. J. Bettis & N. G. Adams (Eds.), *Geographies of girlhood: Identities in-between* (pp. 35–52). Mahwah, NJ: Lawrence Erlbaum Associates.

Johansen, A., Little, S. G., & Akin-Little, A. (2011). An examination of New Zealand teachers' attributions and perceptions of behaviour, classroom management, and the level of formal teacher training received in behaviour management. *Kairaranga, 12*(2), 3–12.

Kounin, J. S., & Obradovik, S. (1967). Managing emotionally disturbed children in regular classrooms: A replication and extension. *Journal of Special Education, 2*(2), 129–135.

Meyer, H. A., Astor, R. A., & Behre, W. J. (2004). Teachers' reasoning about school fights, contexts, and gender: An expanded cognitive developmental approach. *Aggression and Violent Behavior, 9*(1), 45–74.

Monroe, A. E., Blackwell, S. E., & Pepper, S. K. (2010). Strengthening professional development partnerships while bridging classroom management instruction and practice. *The Professional Educator, 34*(2).

Pearl, R., Man-Chi, L., Van Acker, R., Farmer, T., & Rodkin, P. C. (2007). Fourth- and fifth-grade teachers' awareness of their classrooms' social networks. *Elementary School Journal, 108*(1), 25–39.

Simonsen, B., Fairbanks, S., Briesch, A., Myers, D., & Sugai, G. (2008). Evidence based practices in classroom management: Considerations for research to practice. *Education and Treatment of Children, 31*(3), 351–380.

Stormshak, E. A., Bierman, K. L., Bruschi, C., Dodge, K. A., Coie, J. D., & The Conduct Problems Prevention Research Group. (1999). The relation between behavior problems and peer preference in different classroom contexts. *Child Development, 70*(1), 169–182.

Ullucci, K. (2009). "This has to be family": Humanizing classroom management in urban schools. *Journal of Classroom Interaction, 44*(1), 13–28.

Chapter 3

Becoming Teacher Educators

Transformational Journeys of Classroom Teachers

Nancy P. Gallavan

ABSTRACT

Educator preparation program accreditation and teacher education standards advocate that teacher candidates experience a variety of diverse field experiences with highly qualified classroom teachers to serve as their mentors. However, highly qualified classroom teachers may not be prepared to mentor teacher candidates with the purposes, principles, and practices significant to each candidate's future sustained professional success and personal satisfaction.

To explore these concerns, 10 university instructors teaching courses and supervising teacher candidates during field experiences at one institution reflected on their perceptions as both mentor classroom teachers and university instructors providing insights and inspiration for improving the field experiences incorporated into their own educator preparation program. Implications from this study map the transformational journeys experienced by teacher educators who have transitioned from classroom teachers to university instructors and generated pragmatic recommendations useful to educator preparation programs.

KEYWORDS

associated teacher educators, educator preparation programs, teacher self-efficacy, mentor classroom teachers, university instructors

Grace had taught middle school for eight years. Since earning her undergraduate degree to become a classroom teacher specializing in math and social studies education, she had returned to the same university to earn a master's degree in curriculum and instruction with an emphasis on educational technology. Her goal was to become the best classroom teacher possible, not only for her middle-level learners, their families, and her colleagues—especially new teachers—but also for the many university teacher candidates placed in her classroom to complete their field experiences.

After completing her master's degree, Grace began to realize that she was becoming a teacher educator; she enjoyed the opportunities to guide and support candidates and novices in their quest to become effective classroom teachers.

Then the department chair from the university where Grace earned her degrees contacted her asking if she would be interested in applying for a full-time instructor position. In addition to teaching courses, Grace would be responsible for supervising teacher candidates during their field experiences. Wanting to become a university instructor teacher educator to promote personal growth, professional development, and pedagogical expertise, Grace accepted the position.

However, during her first semester at the university she discovered that the classroom teachers with whom teacher candidates were placed for their field experiences were not prepared for mentoring the candidates with the purposes, practices, and professionalism that Grace incorporated into her repertoire or that candidates needed in order to be effective.

Grace acknowledged that she had embarked on her journey in her transformation from classroom teacher to university instructor teacher educator. Now her goals were to help prepare, guide, and support the mentor classroom teachers who were, in actuality, associated teacher educators.

INTRODUCTION

The preparation of teachers requires guidance and support from two groups of teacher educators: university instructors who share the purposes, principles, and practices through well-developed curriculum, instruction, and assessment founded on information and intentionality (Malle, Moses, & Baldwin, 2001), and classroom teachers who share practices, professionalism, and persistence through experiences and mentorship founded on perspectives and positionality (Takas, 2002). However, mentor classroom teachers are not viewed as teacher educators; they do not tend to view themselves as teacher educators.

In this research, 10 university instructors who recently taught in K-12 classrooms and mentored teacher candidates provide insights and inspiration to strengthen their teacher preparation program and relationships with their partners in K-12 schools.

EDUCATOR PREPARATION PROGRAMS AND ATE STANDARDS

Accredited educator preparation programs across the United States such as the Council of Accreditation for Educator Preparation, require their teacher candidates to spend concentrated amounts of high-quality time in appropriate K-12 classrooms as they prepare for their future careers (CAEP, 2013). Typically, candidates visit specific classrooms either individually or with partners early in their programs to conduct observations of the teachers and students; the goals of the observations are for candidates to increase their educator awareness by connecting the concepts attained in their courses with the natural sociocultural context in contemporary classrooms and schools.

As candidates continue in their programs, usually they are placed individually in K-12 classrooms for longer amounts of time to learn from the classroom teacher and to start teaching individual students, small groups, and even the whole class. Now the goals are to engage in authentic application of isolated learning experiences by following the teacher's instructions and modeling.

Finally, candidates, now called interns, are placed in classrooms for a whole semester or a year, perhaps in the same classroom or school where prior observations or placements occurred. The goals of these placements are to experience the holistic advancement transitioning from student to teacher responsible for all aspects of the teaching, learning, and schooling.

"Field experiences have been considered the most important and powerful components of teacher education" (McIntyre, Byrd, & Foxx, 1996, p. 173). During field experiences, teacher candidates are provided opportunities to apply purposes, principles, and practices emphasized in university courses to the practices, professionalism, and persistence modeled in K-12 classrooms. Essential to the conversation of educator preparation is the understanding that both university instructors and classroom teachers are teacher educators.

The Association of Teacher Educators (ATE) defines a teacher educator as anyone who educates teachers (ATE, 1996); to advance the responsibilities shared by both university instructors and classroom teachers, ATE has written standards to promote more effective practices (ATE, 2000). Ultimately, accomplished teacher educators in all settings are expected to fulfill the stipulated indicators documented by various artifacts as evidence of their significant contributions to the preparation of teacher candidates.

Obstacles Related to Mentor Classroom Teachers

Although teacher candidates are taught formally by university instructors, the coursework at the institution emphasizing the purposes, principles, and practices of teaching, learning, and schooling encompasses only half of educator preparation. The other half of preparation relies upon K-12 teachers who are willing to share their classrooms, experience, and expertise as mentors to teacher candidates. However, mentor classroom teachers may not be prepared with the practices, professionalism, and persistence that the educator preparation program expects for candidates to acquire and demonstrate in order to become effective classroom teachers.

Four overarching obstacles occur that teacher educators—university instructors and mentor classroom teachers alike—should acknowledge when placing candidates in classrooms:

Poverty of practice. Extending the findings of Black and Wiliam (1998) that they applied to their research on classroom assessments, the concept of poverty of practice underscores the research on mentoring. Most classroom teachers receive little to no professional development for mentoring teacher candidates. The expectation to mentor effectively is based primarily on the classroom teacher's acquired knowledge and experience in the classroom along with the classroom teacher's availability and interest in hosting a teacher candidate in his or her classroom.

Consequently, many teacher candidates are placed with mentor classroom teachers who are ill-equipped as effective partners in educator preparation. "Simply declaring teachers to be teacher educators or mentors, as is so often done, and occasionally meeting with them on campus to discuss problems and programs does very little to improve the situation" (Bullough, 2005, p. 144).

Apprenticeship of observation. Lortie (1975) established the understanding that teachers learn by observing teachers. This finding contributes to the justification for educator preparation programs to collaborate with mentor classroom teachers to teach teacher candidates during their field places. Yet, in juxtaposition, this finding also illustrates the continuous cycle of mentor classroom teachers advising teacher candidates based on limited information and biased instincts gained predominantly from their own observations and experiences, which may constitute a repertoire of ineffective teaching.

Mewborn and Tyminski (2006) ascertain that cultural transmission and the cycle of ineffective teaching can be disrupted by both the mentor classroom teacher and the teacher candidate. With guidance and support, the mentor classroom teacher can experience new learning that is continuous, productive, and dynamic (Feimen-Nemser, 2001).

Generational perpetuation of practice. Mentor classroom teachers tend to teach and model only the knowledge, skills, and dispositions that they know and value (Gallavan, 2007). Too often, mentor classroom teachers have developed routines and assembled repertoires that may not be current or complete.

Sayeksi and Paulsen (2012) found from their survey research conducted with more than 400 teacher candidates after completing their internships that not all effective classroom teachers are effective mentors and yet only effective classroom teachers can be effective mentors. Although the belief is that experienced classroom teachers offer expertise, too often their routines and repertoires may have become unstructured and incoherent with the passage of time (Zeichner, 2010).

Establishment of relationships. The process of becoming a teacher is a sociocultural experience involving the establishment of many different relationships (Feimen-Nemser, 2001) offering opportunities manifesting both beneficial and detrimental outcomes. Teacher candidates can readily expand their understanding and gain many unanticipated advantages by interacting professionally among the school community to glean an array of positive and productive practices (Gallavan & Benson, 2014).

Conversely, teacher candidates may reap fewer advantages or even disadvantageous results by aligning themselves with only a few professionals, especially unconstructive and/or negative individuals (Sinclair, Dowson, & Thistleton-Martin, 2006). The sociocultural context of the K-12 classrooms encompasses nested communities within schools, neighborhoods, districts, states, and so forth, with whom the teacher candidate should interact.

However, the mentor classroom teacher serves as the gatekeeper who opens the gates to new opportunities for the teacher candidate. The teacher educator depends on the mentor classroom teacher to legitimize the placement and provide access to beneficial relationships and outcomes (Cuenca, 2011).

Ultimately, by chance and by choice, teacher candidates are placed with mentor classroom teachers who may or may not be prepared to mentor. Both intentionality and positionality must be considered when placing teacher candidates with mentor classroom teachers whose practices range in effectiveness for both K-12 student and teacher candidate learning.

CLASSROOM TEACHERS AS ASSOCIATED TEACHER EDUCATORS

Currently, 3.1 million teachers comprise the U.S. teaching workforce (NCES, 2015). In the next 10 years, approximately 1.5 million new teachers will enter U.S. classrooms (DeMonte, 2015). These numbers make visible the need for educator preparation programs to strengthen their field placements addressing the quality of both the expectations and the mentoring.

Given that mentor classroom teachers are not viewed nor view themselves as teacher educators, efforts dedicated to the roles and responsibilities of mentor classroom teachers (Lu, 2010; Murray, 2013) could transform the current view so mentor classroom teachers become associated teacher educators and, thus, serve as equal partners in educator preparation programs.

Specifically, mentor classroom teachers' need to increase their awareness of the presence and power of the four sources of teacher self-efficacy and their corresponding roles and responsibilities for featuring the four sources in developmentally appropriate ways during the field experiences is essential. Only in the classroom can teacher candidates fully understand and appreciate the four sources of teacher self-efficacy corresponding to the four stages of modeling, messages, mediation, and mentoring. Bandura (1977) identified the four sources of self-efficacy:

(1) vicarious observations involve watching the expert in action, being guided in isolated student interactions, engaging in journey writing, receiving general feedback, and are expected to occur during the First Placement;
(2) verbal persuasion involves being guided in initial teaching, engaging in initial reflection, receiving specific feedback, and are expected to occur during the First and Second Placements;
(3) physiological feedback involves taking limited responsibility in teaching and learning, engaging in new found reflection, receiving honest feedback, and are expected to occur during the Second and Third Placements; and
(4) mastery experiences involve taking full responsibility for teaching and learning, engaging in meaningful reflection, receiving critical feedback, and are expected to occur during the Third Placement.

As educator preparation programs seek ways to modify their approaches to ensure quality field experiences emphasizing teacher self-efficacy, research conducted with former mentor classroom teachers, such as the findings reported here, yields recommendations for both immediate and long-range possibilities for change.

METHODOLOGY

This study was conducted at a mid-sized university located in the mid-south United States to investigate the following research question: How can the faculty teaching and supervising in one specific educator preparation program improve the preparation, support, and guidance of the mentor classroom teachers with whom teacher candidates are placed for their field experiences to improve the quality of their field experiences?

To investigate this question, a survey was conducted with a specific group of participants. The survey research used in this study allowed participants to reflect on their unique experiences and to construct their distinct responses, crafting comprehensive descriptions relevant to each survey item. Time and space were allowed for participants to respond fully accommodating their individual schedules and narrative lengths.

Participants

Participants in this study included 10 instructors currently teaching courses and supervising teacher candidates in various field experiences in one specific educator preparation program. Each participant had been employed as a classroom teacher within the past 10 years at a middle level or high school located within the geographic area that their educator preparation program serves. These criteria were established to identify specific participants in order to gain information related directly to their educator preparation program to improve the preparation, guidance, and support of their mentor classroom teachers.

Survey

The survey shown in Figure 3.1 was distributed electronically via Qualtrics. Participants were informed in advance that the survey would require approximately 20–30 minutes and that gift bags would be placed in the department workroom as expressions of appreciation for their participation. Participants also were informed of the researcher conducting the investigation and the availability of the researcher to receive additional commentary via e-mail message or office conversation.

Data Analysis

Data were analyzed using narrative enquiry clarifying thematic, structural, dialogic, and visual aspects (Riessman, 2007). Through narrative enquiry, participants provided their reflections describing their unique experiences, which produced insights and inspiration to improve the placements of teacher candidates during field experiences and the relationships with mentor classroom teachers. This study relied on narrative enquiry examining the reflections shared by the participants as part of their transformational journeys as teacher educators moving from classroom teacher to university instructor (Webster & Mertova, 2007).

Analyses (Russell & Berry, 2012) of the narratives revealed (a) overarching themes or continuous threads conveying meanings similar among the other people's narratives; (b) fundamental structures constructed to identify,

Mark the response that best describes you.
1. I have taught middle level or high school. ○ Yes ○ No
2. I teach courses and supervise teacher candidates. ○ Yes ○ No

(Automatic Removal) By marking "No" to 1 or 2, then you do not match the desired population sought complete this survey. Thank you~

~~~~~~

3. I am ○ Female ○ Male
4. I am ○ African-American
○ Asian-American
○ Caucasian
○ Latina/o
○ Native American
○ Other: (explain)
5. I taught middle level or high school classes as a licensed classroom teacher for
○ 1 year
○ 2 years
○ 3 years
○ 4 years
○ 5 years
○ More than 5 years
6. As a classroom teacher, was a college/university teacher candidate placed in your classroom to complete a required field experience? ○ Yes ○ No
7. As a classroom teacher, were you prepared, guided, and/or supported to mentor a teacher candidate completing a field experience before the placement began, at any time the candidate was placed in your classroom, and/or after the placement ended?
○ Yes ○ No
8. If you answered item #7 as "Yes," please describe the preparation, guidance, and/or support.
9. Describe a time when a teacher candidate was placed in your classroom (for any capacity) and your experiences.
10. When the teacher candidate was placed in your classroom for any field experience, did the candidate seem sure, somewhat sure, or unsure of the educator preparation expectations. (Mark only one answer). ○ Sure ○ Somewhat Sure ○ Unsure
11. When the teacher candidate was placed in your classroom for any field experience, did the candidate seem displeased or pleased? (Mark only one answer).
○ Displeased ○ Pleased
12. When the teacher candidate was placed in your classroom for any field experience, did the candidate seem reluctant or eager? (Mark only one answer).
○ Reluctant ○ Eager
13. At any time as a classroom teacher mentoring teacher candidates, did you seek additional information from the Internet, published materials, i.e., books, journals, magazines, colleagues, and/or professional development opportunities?
14. If you answered item #10 as "Yes," please describe your activities.
15. At any time as a classroom teacher mentoring teacher educators or novice teachers did you think of yourself as becoming a teacher educator? ○ Yes ○ No
16. If you answered item #12 as "Yes," please describe your thoughts.
17. If you answered item #12 as "No," please describe reasons you did not think of yourself as a teacher educator.
18. Describe the factors that influenced your transformation from classroom teacher to teacher educator including the people who influenced your decisions and transformation.
19. As a teacher educator, reflect on your years as a classroom teacher and describe the knowledge, skills, and dispositions you now possess that you wish you had possessed as a classroom teacher related to mentoring teacher candidates.
20. As a teacher educator, reflect on your current practices and describe the knowledge, skills, and dispositions that you share (or your program shares) with classroom teachers who mentor teacher candidates.
21. As a teacher educator, reflect on your current practices, and describe the knowledge, skills, and dispositions that you *would like* to share (or you *would like* your program to share) with classroom teachers who mentor teacher candidates.
22. Think about contemporary educator preparation programs. Describe the ideal approaches and rationale for the preparation, guidance, and support of mentor classroom teachers.
23. Think about contemporary educator preparation programs. Describe the consequences for empowering and equipping classroom teachers to mentor teacher candidates and, consequently, promote their transition in becoming teacher educators.
24. What additional recommendations would you make to strengthen quality field experiences for educator preparation programs?

Figure 3.1 Survey Distributed via Qualtrics

describe, rationalize, and justify the narratives; (c) contextual dialogic communicating the sociocultural context depicting the situation; and (d) the reported albeit interpreted reflections communicated in the narratives.

Findings

Ten instructors teaching courses and supervising teaching candidates in one educator preparation program participated in this study and completed the survey. Seven of the participants sent additional e-mail messages most of which expressed appreciation for gathering these data.

One e-mail communicated more information to be added to a survey item response. Three of the participants (none of whom sent e-mail messages) visited with the researcher to discuss their survey item responses. Given that this survey was conducted in one educator preparation program and the name of the researcher was shared with the participants, the researcher anticipated follow-up e-mail messages and office conversations.

Of the 10 survey participants, 9 were female and 1 was male; 1 was African-American, 0 were Asian-American, 7 were Caucasian, 1 was Latina, and 1 was bi-racial. Of the 10 survey participants, 1 had taught for 4 years, 1 had taught for 5 years, and 8 had taught more than 5 years. As classroom teachers, all 10 survey participants had had a teacher candidate placed in their classroom to complete a required field experience.

All 10 survey participants responded that they had been prepared, guided, and/or supported in some way. However, their descriptions explained that they had received some form of information via the teacher candidate regarding the expectations, amount of time, necessary forms to be completed, and so on. None of the survey participants reported preparation other than being asked if they would like to mentor a teacher candidate or were informed that they would be mentoring a teacher candidate.

For all survey participants, the invitation or the assignment to mentor was extended with short notice, as short as one day. None of the 10 survey participant reported any additional guidance, and support was provided before, during, and/or after the placement of the teacher candidate by the educator preparation program.

The descriptions of the teacher candidate placements provided rich and varied accounts. Two overarching themes were identified for each of the three field experience placements among the participants' descriptions:

First Placement-Observation

    a. Teacher candidates were unsure of their educator preparation program expectations, seemed pleased to visit the classroom, yet reluctant to interact with students.

    b. Teacher candidates were somewhat sure of their educator preparation program expectations, seemed pleased to visit the classroom, and were eager to interact with students.

Second Placement-Initial Teaching

    a. Teacher candidates were unsure of their educator preparation program expectations, seemed pleased to learn from their mentors, and were reluctant to start teaching lesson.

    b. Teacher candidates were somewhat sure of their educator preparation program expectations, were pleased to learn from their mentors, and were eager to start teaching lessons.

Third Placement-Internship

    a. Teacher candidates were unsure of their educator preparation program expectations, were pleased to learn from their mentors, and seemed reluctant to take full responsibility.

    b. Teacher candidates were somewhat sure of their educator preparation program expectations, were pleased to learn from their mentors, and were eager to take full responsibility.

However, some survey participants also described situations where teacher candidates who had been assigned to their First Placements were not sure if their teacher candidates were pleased or displeased to be assigned to a classroom. This finding suggests that these teacher candidates were not convinced that they actually wanted to become classroom teachers or were just visiting the classroom as a career option.

All 10 of the survey participants reported that they sought additional information relevant to mentoring teaching candidates via the Internet; no professional development was reported. Four of the 10 survey participants reported that they thought of themselves as becoming teacher educators. One survey participant wrote:

> *An intern told me that I knew much more about teaching than her professors at the university and that I taught her in ways that she had never been taught. She told me that I made teaching and learning much more meaningful and real. At that moment, I wondered what was required to teach at the university and what that kind of career would be like. I began daydreaming about the perfect way to prepare a teacher.*

Six of the 10 survey participants reported that they did not think of themselves as teacher educators. One survey participant wrote:

> *I volunteered to have teacher candidates placed in my classroom. I thought I was an effective teacher, I liked teaching, and I would be a career classroom teacher. But I never viewed myself as a teacher educator.*

The survey participants described many different factors that influenced their transformation from classroom teacher to teacher educator that included:

- *I found myself looking critically at my classroom from the perspective of the placed teacher candidate. Did I model the most effective practices to prepare the teacher candidate for a classroom teaching position?*
- *After a teacher candidate asked me why I taught the way I taught, I realized that I did not really know the answer other than I had acquired the practice from another teacher . . . probably my own mentor classroom teachers. I wanted to understand the research behind my practices.*
- *My intern was required to visit other classrooms. Then we talked about the similarities and differences. I wished I had the opportunity to visit other teacher's classrooms to learn new practices. I decided that I either needed to make that happen at school or find a different way to expand my strategies.*

When reflecting on their years as classroom teachers, the survey participants described a range of knowledge, skills, and dispositions they now possess but wished they had possessed when mentor teacher candidates that included:

- *As I classroom teacher, I aligned my lessons and units with the content standards. Now as a university instructor, I know there are many other standards that a classroom teacher should fulfill.*
- *I was mostly concerned with my teaching; only after becoming a university instructor did I comprehend my responsibilities related to learning. The idea of self-efficacy was unclear to me so I avoided those conversations. I get it now.*
- *I did not realize how isolated I felt as a classroom teacher. The time spent with other classroom teachers was dedicated to scheduling or socializing. Rarely did we actually plan curriculum, instruction, or assessments. We are much more collaborative as university instructors.*

The survey items probing the knowledge, skills, dispositions that they currently share, as well as the knowledge, skills, and dispositions that they would like to share with classroom teachers who mentor teacher candidates gleaned valuable insights that included:

Currently Share—

- *I tell the mentor classroom teacher to allow the teacher candidate to teach as much as possible and as soon as possible. Observing needs to be reduced quickly each day to optimize the teacher candidate's time in the classroom.*

- *The mentor classroom teacher must let the teacher candidate plan the learning and then teach the lesson early in the placement. The teacher candidate needs to experience both the strengths and weaknesses of the lesson so the candidate can internalize the necessity of modifying. Too often teacher candidates falsely presume that every lesson will be perfect and be taught the same way forever.*
- *Give the teacher candidate honest objective feedback frequently. Honest feedback should be a balance of effectiveness that is celebrated and ineffectiveness that must be changed. Feedback should be shared in ways that professional and not interpreted as personal. Talk about the behavior and not the person.*

Would Like to Share—

- *Do not require the teacher candidate to prepare materials in the workroom, grade papers, take responsibility for a monitoring duty, etc., in your place. Unless you are fulfilling these tasks, your teacher candidate should not do them for you.*
- *Avoid the negative conversations about students, their families, other teachers, community members, etc., that often are heard in the teachers' lounge and other locations. Actions speak much louder than words.*
- *Be aware of your attitudes towards the students. You may (intentionally or unintentionally) show biasness and prejudice toward particular students or groups of students.*

Finally, the last two items on the survey revealed the ideal approaches and rationale related to the preparation, guidance, and support of mentor classroom teachers as well as the consequences for empowering and equipping classroom teachers to mentor teacher candidates and, consequently, promote their transition in becoming teacher educators.

Implications

The implications of this study are clear. Educator preparation programs must collaborate with mentor classroom teachers in ways that are honest, natural, authentic, and holistic. Placed teacher candidates need to be involved in the conversations so they are sure of their program expectations; be equipped with the developmentally appropriate knowledge, skills, and dispositions relevant to the classroom placement (observation, initial teaching and learning, internship); and be empowered to experience effectiveness in the classroom so they understand the significance of their endeavors and achieve success and satisfaction that can be sustained throughout their careers.

Concurrently, mentor classroom teachers must be involved in the conversations and decisions to accept a placed teacher candidates in their classrooms, be prepared with the developmentally appropriate knowledge, skills, and dispositions for interacting with placed teacher candidates; and be empowered to experience effectiveness as an associated teacher educator so they understand the significance of their endeavors and achieve success and satisfaction that can be sustained throughout their careers either in the classroom or as a teacher educator teaching and supervising in an educator preparation program.

Thus, educator preparation programs and the school districts where teacher candidates are placed should form partnerships that oversee these essential experiences as emphasized in the CAEP Standard 2 (2013). Teacher educators situated on university campuses should be present in schools and classrooms; mentor classroom teachers, aka associated teacher educators, should be present on university campuses as shown in Figure 3.2.

The dichotomy of "us" and "them" does not enhance either the educator preparation or the relationship between K-12 schools and universities.

Recommendations

The results of this study reveal 10 recommendations for educator education programs to consider in the preparation, guidance, and support of their mentor classroom teachers with whom teacher candidates are placed for their field experiences.

1. The mentor classroom teacher should have completed at least 3 years of documented effective teaching, learning, and schooling in the grade level(s) and academic subject area(s) where the teacher candidate will be placed.
2. The mentor classroom teacher should be involved in conversations with the school administrator responsible for making the teacher candidate field experience placements.

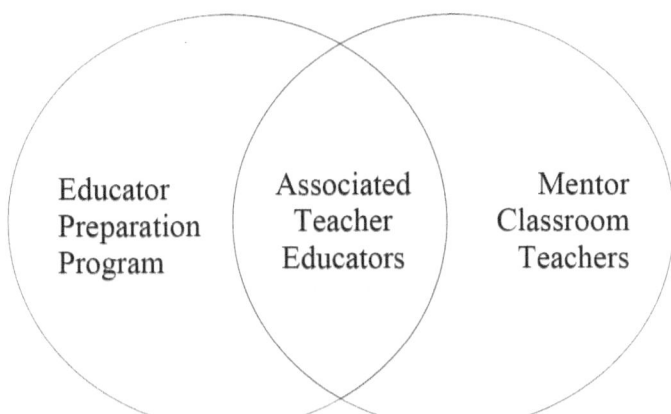

Figure 3.2   Classroom Teachers as Associated Teacher Educators

3. The mentor classroom teacher should have completed a professional development course provided by the educator preparation program as preparation before a teacher candidate is placed in his or her classroom. The professional development course may be available via online, face-to-face, or hybrid format.
4. The mentor classroom teacher should be provided additional professional development by the educator preparation program as guidance and support during and after the completion of the teacher candidate field experience placement. Guidance and support may be available via online, face-to-face, or hybrid format in additional to continuous availability via e-mail and telephone.
5. The mentor classroom teacher should be provided resources offering theory, research, practices, and collegiality available as a website maintained by the educator preparation program. Opportunities for classroom mentor teachers to submit blog postings (monitored by the educator preparation program) should be available.
6. The mentor classroom teacher should be offered opportunities to be mentored as an associated teacher educator. Some mentor classroom teachers may recognize their transformation to becoming a teacher educator and would welcome opportunities to advance their knowledge, skills, and dispositions in the classroom, within a school district, with the state department of education, at a university, and so on.
7. Teacher educators teaching and supervising in the educator preparation program should develop specific expectations to be communicated with the mentor classroom teachers, the school administrators making the placements, and the teacher candidates when candidates are placed for their first classroom field experiences, that is, observations.
8. Teacher educators teaching and supervising in the educator preparation program should develop specific expectations to be communicated with the mentor classroom teachers, the school administrators making the placements, and the teacher candidates when candidates are placed for their second classroom field experiences, that is, initial teaching and teacher responsibilities.
9. Teacher educators teaching and supervising in the educator preparation program should develop specific expectations to be communicated with the mentor classroom teachers, the school administrator making the placements, and the teacher candidates when candidates are placed for their third classroom field experiences, that is, internships.
10. Teacher educators teaching and supervising in the educator preparation program should develop specific expectations to be documented as part of the education preparation program for continuous assessment, data collection, analysis, and revision.

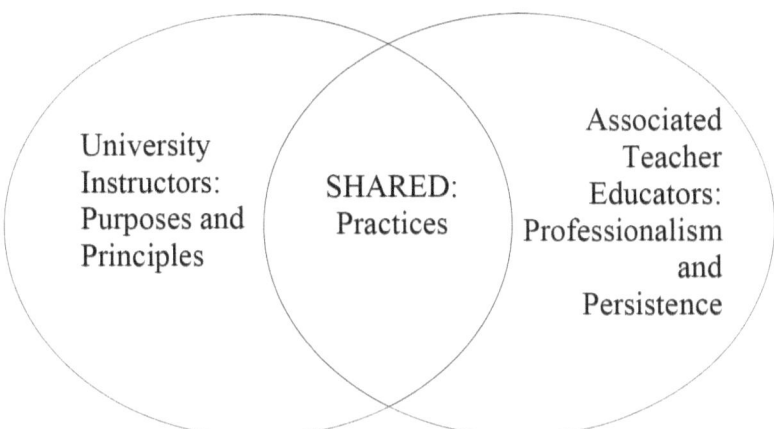

Figure 3.3 Shared Partnership Between University Instructors and Associated Teacher Educators.

CONCLUSIONS

Given that the most important element in a student's education is the effective teacher (Darling-Hammond, 2006), then it appears that the most important element in an educator's preparation is the effective mentor classroom teacher (Korth & Baum, 2011). Quality field experiences are extremely important in teacher preparation (Baum & Korth, 2013). This study shows the reciprocity between evidence-based practices (required by the educator preparation program) and the practice-based evidence (produced by the mentor classroom teacher).

The ultimate outcome should be collaborative partnerships that ensure that the preparation of classroom teachers encompasses the purposes, principles, practices, professionalism, and persistence required of all teachers (see Figure 3.3).

REFERENCES

Association of Teacher Educators (ATE). (1996). Standards for Teacher Educators. Retrieved from http://www.ate1.org/pubs/uploads/tchredstds0308.pdf

Association of Teacher Educator (ATE). (2000). Standards for Field Experiences in Teacher Education. Retrieved from http://www.ate1.org/pubs/uploads/nfdfstds.pdf

Bandura, A. (1977). Self-efficacy: Toward a unifying theory of behavioral change. *Psychological Review, 84*(2), 191–215.

Baum, A. C., & Korth, B. B. (2013). Preparing classroom teachers to be cooperating teachers: A report of current efforts, beliefs, challenges, and associated recommendations. *Journal of Early Childhood Education, 34*, 171–190.

Black, P., & Wiliam, D. (1998). Assessment and classroom learning. *Educational Assessment: Principles, Policy, and Practice, 5*(1), 7–74.

Bullough, R. V., Jr. (2005). Being and becoming a mentor: School-based teacher educators and teacher educator identity. *Teaching and Teacher Education, 21*, 143–155.

Council for Accreditation of Educator Preparation (CAEP). (2013). Accreditation standards. Retrieved from http://caepnet.org/2013/08/29/new-accreditation-standards-adopted/

Cuenca, A. (2011). The role of legitimacy in student teaching: Learning to "feel" like a teacher. *Teacher Education Quarterly, 38*(2), 117–130.

Feimen-Nemser, S. (2001). From preparation to practice: Designing a continuum to strengthen and sustain teaching. *Teachers College Record, 106*(6), 1013–1055.

Darling-Hammond, L. (2006). Constructing 21st century teacher education. *Journal of Teacher Education, 57*(3), 300–314.

DeMonte, J. (2015). A Million new teachers are coming; Will they be ready to teach? Educational Policy Center at American Institutes for Research. Retrieved from http://educationpolicy.air.org/sites/default/files/Brief-MillionNewTeachers.pdf

Gallavan, N. P. (2007). Seven perceptions that influence novice teachers' efficacy and cultural competence. *Journal of Praxis in Multicultural Education, 2*(1), 6–22.

Gallavan, N. P., & Benson, T. R. (2014). Getting on the same PAGE: Illuminating teacher candidates' paths with customized student support services. In N. P. Gallavan & L. G. Putney (Eds.), *ATE Yearbook XXIII Optimizing teaching, learning, and schooling with classroom assessment, program evaluation, and educator accountability* (pp. 490–502). Philadelphia, PA: Taylor & Francis.

Korth, B. B., & Baum, A. (2011). Teachers supporting future teachers: A critical part of early childhood teacher preparation. *Young Children, 66*, 20–26.

Lortie, D. (1975). *Schoolteacher: A sociological study*. Chicago, IL: University of Chicago Press.

Lu, H.-L. (2010). Building a rationale for cooperating teaching training: A phenomenological study. *National Teacher Education Journal, 3*(2) 13–32.

Malle, B. F., Moses, L. J., & Baldwin, D. A. (2001). Introduction: The significance of intentionality. In B. F. Malle, L. J. Moses, & D. A. Baldwin (Eds.), *Intentions and intentionality: Foundations of social cognition* (pp. 1–24). Cambridge, MA: MIT Press.

McIntyre, D. J., Byrd, D. M., & Foxx, S. M. (1996). Field and laboratory experiences. In J. Sikula, T. J. Buttery, & E. Guyton (Eds.), *Handbook on research in teacher education* (2nd ed., pp. 171–193). New York, NY: Macmillan.

Mewborn, D. S., & Tyminski, A. M. (2006). Lortie's apprenticeship of observation revisited. *For the Learning of Mathematics, 26*(3), 30–33.

Murray, F. B. (2013). Cooperating teachers' evaluation of accredited teacher education programs. *Teacher Education and Practice, 26*(3), 542–553.

National Center for Educational Statistics (NCES). (2015). Fast facts. Institution of educational sciences. Retrieved from http://nces.ed.gov/fastfacts/display.asp?id=372

Riessman, C. K. (2007). *Narrative methods for the human sciences*. Thousand Oaks, CA: Sage.

Russell, T., & Berry, A. (2012). Self-study and the development of new perspectives on pre-service teacher education. *Studying Teacher Education: Journal of Self-Study of Teacher Education Practices, 8*(2), 105–107.

Sayeski, K. L., & Paulsen, K. J. (2012). Student teacher evaluations of cooperating teachers as indices of effective mentoring. *Teacher Education Quarterly, 39*(2), 117–130.

Sinclair, C., Dowson, M., & Thistleton-Martin, J. (2006). Motivations and profiles of cooperating teachers: Who volunteers and why? *Teaching and Teacher Education, 22*(3), 263–279.

Takas, D. (2002). Positionality, epistemology, and social justice in the classroom. *Social Justice, 29*(4), 168–181.

Webster, L., & Mertova, P. (2007). *Using narrative inquiry as a research method: An introduction to using critical event narrative analysis in research on learning and teaching*. New York, NY: Routledge.

Zeichner, K. (2010). Rethinking the connections between campus courses and field experiences in college-and university-based teacher education. *Journal of Teacher Education, 61*(1), 89–99.

Chapter 4

Learning from Experience

Insights from Veteran Classroom Teachers on Teacher Preparation

Louise Ammentorp

ABSTRACT

Since 2002, when No Child Left Behind became law, the field of education has experienced seemingly constant changes in curriculum, instruction, and the tests used to evaluate students. The implementation of the Common Core Standards, and the accompanying tests, has exacerbated these challenges. By developing reciprocal collaborative relationships with the teachers who mentor our students, university-based teacher educators can more effectively prepare preservice teachers for the challenges of today's classrooms.

This chapter presents discussions with six veteran elementary school teachers who share their experience mentoring preservice teachers in their classroom. Through semi-structured interviews with the author, a university-based teacher educator, the teachers offer insight into the common struggles of preservice teachers. The teachers offer valuable suggestions for preservice teachers and university-based teacher educators.

KEYWORDS

associated teacher educators, clinical experience, collaboration, preservice teachers, teacher preparation, veteran teachers

Connecting coursework and field experience is one of the more difficult challenges facing teacher education programs (Darling-Hammond, 2006; Darling-Hammond, Hammerness, Grossman, Rust, & Shulman, 2005; Feiman-Nemser & Buchmann, 1985; Zeichner, 2010). In recognition of this problem, the National Council for Accreditation of Teacher Education (NCATE) issued a report (2010) calling for teacher education model to be "turned upside down," with a renewed focus on school-based field experiences.

Strong clinical practice has been linked to student achievement, teacher retention, and teachers' sense of preparedness (American Association of Colleges for Teacher Education [AACTE], 2010). However, more field experience isn't necessarily better (Association of Teacher Educators [ATE], 2000). The quality of the mentorship (university supervisor and cooperating teacher), the school placement, and the relationship between the university and schools are all important aspects of clinical experience (ATE, 2008; Grossman, 2010).

The creation of field-based learning spaces that respect the experience and knowledge of classroom teachers is crucial to the development and education of preservice teachers (Feiman-Nemser & Beasley, 2007; Zeichner, 2010).

The ATE Standards for Teacher Educators (ATE, 2008) state that accomplished teacher educators model best practices (Standard 1) and collaborate (Standard 6). To meet these standards, university-based teacher educators cannot approach working with classroom teachers from a "deficit model" (Feiman-Nemser, 1998; Zeichner, 2010). While there is a need for supporting teachers in their development as effective mentors (Bullough, 2005; Feiman-Nemser, 2001; Gardiner, 2009; Young, Bullough, Draper, Smith, & Erickson, 2005), the focus should not be how to bring college knowledge and professional development to teachers (Zeichner, 2010).

Instead, it should involve reciprocal discussions between university teacher educators and the school-based associated teacher educators on how to best to prepare preservice teachers (Bullough, 2005; Young et al., 2005). In other words, classroom teachers should be considered colleagues and peers— "associated teacher educators" (ATE, n.d.). Associated teacher educators offer insight and expertise that is different from the instruction of university-based educators, especially given the rapid changes in schools in the past few years. Veteran teachers have endured continual change in curriculum and instruction since 2002.

In particular, the emphasis on data-driven assessments and their analysis creates additional layers of new kinds of teacher work beyond the traditional day-to-day demands. This knowledge and experience is unique to classroom teachers working in the schools. It is essential that preservice teachers have opportunities to learn these aspects of teaching while still in their teacher preparation programs. As a university-based teacher educator and former classroom teacher, the author supervises preservice teachers in their clinical placements.

After working with some of the same teachers over the years, the author began to recognize just how many schools are changing and how much the author relies on teachers and her own field supervision to keep knowledge up to date. In particular, the role of collaboration is much more prominent in schools than when the author was a classroom teacher. Effective teachers are expert communicators and collaborators (Darling-Hammond, 2006). They collaborate with each other, with special education teachers, with other specialists, with parents, and with administrators.

The preparation of teachers, therefore, involves the development of "soft" skills such as self-regulation, resilience, working with challenging people, collaboration, communication, compromise and acceptance of critical feedback, in addition to content knowledge and instructional methods. However, these skills are often not directly taught, or modeled, within teacher education programs, and particularly not during students' clinical/field experience in the PreK–12 classrooms (Gardiner & Robinson, 2009; Lawley, Moore, & Smajic, 2014).

With this in mind, a colleague and the author began conducting research on student perspectives on the benefits and challenges of collaboration in the context of preservice teachers' paired placements (Ammentorp & Madden, 2014) as well as the development of workplace skills in the clinical setting (Ammentorp & Madden, accepted). It became very clear that the cooperating teachers' perspective was an essential missing piece in our research.

Although the author and cooperating teachers had conversations about the preservice teachers' progress, they never formally discussed the mentoring process. The author had avoided more structured appointments for fear of imposing on their time. The author didn't want to ask more of them as they already gave so much of their time and the stipend they receive for mentoring our students is small.

With so much on their plates, the author was wary of adding more, realizing, however, that they are more than willing to share their expertise, and that their knowledge and experience would benefit not only me and my students, but the teacher education community as a whole.

In this chapter the author shares discussions from her semi-structured interviews with the teachers. The goals for the project included: (a) to gain insight into the teachers' perspective on the challenges preservice teachers face in their clinical placements and the ways teachers assist students in these struggles, (b) to learn the ways they collaborate as teachers, and (c) to use this knowledge to strengthen teacher preparation programs.

CONTEXT AND PARTICIPANTS

The author teaches early childhood and elementary education undergraduate students in a small state college in the Northeastern United States. Students in the program are primarily 18–22 years old, Caucasian and female. The college is known as a highly selective organization, with a 46% acceptance rate and incoming first-year students consistently score greater than 1300 on their verbal and quantitative SAT scores.

As students go through our program, they accumulate field experiences of increasing complexity. Students take courses in blocks to maximize time in the field. They are partnered for their field placements during three semesters in their sophomore and junior years. Prior to their student teaching, the students take their Advance Core Block, a semester-long intensive field-based experience where they are in a school two days a week and two full weeks at the end of the semester. They are partnered for the clinical component of the course, and they plan and teach weekly lessons and develop and teach a 10-lesson unit.

Their instructors for this course are primarily full-time and tenured or tenure track. Students meet two days a week at the college for a seminar. The seminar focuses on instructional methods, such as lesson planning and implementation, differentiation, class management, and designing a unit that they will teach in the field. They are all in the same school for their clinical placement. The university-based professor is on-site and observes their lessons and conferences with them at the school on the days they teach.

The elementary school is in a high-performing suburban district in New Jersey. The six teachers who participated in the structured interviews are all Caucasian females teaching at the school. (See Table 4.1 for more information on teachers.) All names have been changed for confidentiality.

The author conducted three separate interviews, one with three teachers (Janice, Meredith, Amy), one with two teachers (Camille and Karyn), and one with one teacher (Linda). The grouping of the interviews was based

Table 4.1 *Information on Teachers*

Name	# of Years Teaching	#of Semesters Mentoring Students	Grade Currently Teaching
Camille	22	4	2nd
Karyn	18	3	2nd
Janice	20	1	1st
Meredith	19	1	1st
Amy	6	1	K
Linda	30	1	Preschool

solely on their availability. However, since the interviews occurred during their planning time, the schedule led to interviews with grade-based teams (Amy just moved to kindergarten from 1st and was interviewed with her 1st-grade colleagues). Although unintended, this grouping certainly impacted the discussion, especially in regards to teacher collaboration. All interviews were recorded and transcribed.

The research is exploratory in nature, so my analysis focused on emergent themes within and across the interviews. Questions included:

- What do you find are the biggest struggles preservice teachers have in their clinical experience?
- What strategies do you find work in helping them in these challenges?
- What are skills they learn in the classroom setting that are difficult to gain in the college classroom?
- What are ways you collaborate?
- Is there anything you think would be helpful for future teachers to know about mentoring partnered preservice teachers?
- What suggestions do you have for faculty to support your work in mentoring students? and,
- What are ways teacher preparation programs can better prepare students for collaboration and other skills?

VETERAN TEACHER INSIGHTS: COMMON STRUGGLES OF PRESERVICE TEACHERS

Not surprisingly, when discussing the challenges preservice teachers face, the teachers emphasized the logistical aspects of teaching and the ability to go from planning the lesson to teaching it. This includes pacing, time management, class management, and the ability to adapt their lessons on the spot. Our students often come to their first lessons well prepared and practiced for the imagined "perfect" lesson. It is the implementation, however, that is challenging. As Camille points out:

> It seems college is doing a good job of preparing them how to write a lesson plan. Very detailed and what not. However, I sometimes say don't look at that just tell me what you are going to do. Their lesson plan's detail can hinder the natural roll with it, especially if a child doesn't get it.

In her interview, Linda, the special education preschool teacher with over 30 years of experience, agreed that students write excellent plans. She feels being good at paperwork—writing objectives, assessments, and detailed plans is an important skill for teachers coming into the profession today. She expressed concern, however, that they lack "performance" skills. For Linda, teaching is like acting and preservice teachers struggle with the flow and timing of lessons as they enact their "script" on the "stage." This challenge is exacerbated when they either ignore their audience (the children) and/or allow the children (and other observers) to distract them. Similarly, Janice reflected, "they often get caught up in dotting i's and crossing t's and the clock is going." She stressed that preservice teachers have to learn to keep going in a lesson and not to get caught in the ongoing distractions, such as the fire drills, phone ringing, people walking in and out, and of course, the students themselves.

In response to Janice's comments, the rest of the 1st-grade and kindergarten teachers wittily listed a few types of students they encounter during a single lesson: "the toucher," "the talker," "the I don't want to do whatever you tell me to do," "the sleeper," "the I need a tissue," "the one with the tooth that just fell out," "the window looker," "the pencil player," "the pencil dropper," "the desk searcher," "the hungry one," "the crier," "the chair tipper," "the medical emergency complainer," "the bathroom goer," "the tattler," "the pencil sharpener," and "the one asking when is it time to go home?"

And even more types could be added specifically for new preservice teachers: "the supervisor/corrector" ("that isn't how our teacher does it"), "the BFF," and "the hugger" (who starts a receiving line of hugs). Clearly, knowledge of these types is derived from experience.

Learning to prioritize and multitask, knowing when to let things go and when to intervene, and going with, while leading, the flow of a lesson are important teacher skills that come with classroom experience. There are also the more serious disruptive behaviors that teachers encounter, as Linda explains,

> You can talk about behavior until you're blue in the face. Learning at college never, ever, ever prepares you for the classroom when a desk goes flying, when a kid throws himself on the ground or spits at you or says "no!" You cannot teach them that at college they have to learn that on site.

When asked how they support the preservice teachers in overcoming these challenges, the teachers stressed the importance of welcoming them into the classroom and providing ongoing and immediate feedback. They recognized that the preservice teachers often struggle with finding their place in the classroom, particularly since they come once a week at first. Karyn highlighted the role of the teacher in setting the tone of the room and creating a safe place to learn and make mistakes, because mistakes are a part of learning:

> It's something to get across to them that it's not going to go smoothly there are going to be bumps; this is a really hard job to do. We aren't judging you, we are observing giving ideas and advice because of experience but it's safe no one

is expecting you to be perfect. That is not the reality of teaching. The reality of teaching is being reflective enough to say that "well that didn't work at all I really got to do something."

The recognition of the importance of creating a safe space for preservice teachers to make mistakes echoes the findings of Torrez and Krebs (2012). Master mentor teachers in their study considered "opportunity" as the most important characteristic for a quality placement of students. This includes opportunity for making mistakes in a safe space, to build relationships with students, and to participate in all aspects of the teacher experience (such as grade team meetings). The teachers from my study included the preservice teachers in many aspects of their teaching lives.

Even though my students are at the school only one and a half days a week, they are often included in team meetings, field trips, school-wide events, and professional development workshops. They have been invited by the teachers to join the Friday breakfast at the school, to meet for coffee; and they even participated in a professional learning community meeting at one of their houses. The students feel welcome and safe in the classroom and the school as a whole. Everyone is friendly to them (and each other) in the hallway, and the students appreciate and learn from the sense of community.

Karyn goes on to describe how the feeling of safety that the teacher provides for the preservice teachers forms the foundation for the development of self-reflection skills and the ability to accept critical feedback:

> The reflective piece is huge, being open, willing to accept feedback and criticism; being reflective about own teaching; being strong enough to say "that didn't go well" or on the flipside being strong enough to say "that went really well—can I talk about it so maybe you can do it too?" Our school is really great about that open and sharing.

Karyn's words reveal both her insight regarding the mentorship of preservice teachers and her embodiment of the qualities of an effective teacher: in particular, her supporting of students' reflective dialogue and her own practice as a reflective teacher (Feiman-Nesmer, 1998; Young et.al., 2005; Zeichner & Liston, 2014). In fact, all of the cooperating teachers interviewed exhibit (and support in preservice teachers) qualities of exemplar teachers. The teachers' experience, subject knowledge, and pedagogy reflect their strength in educational "human capital" (Hargreaves & Fullan, 2012; Leana, 2011).

Furthermore, the strength of the school's "social capital" (the nature of the interactions and collaboration between teachers) is exceptional as well. According to Leana (2011), the combination of both aspects positively affects student outcomes. Certainly, having experienced associated teacher educators in a collaborative supportive school positively influences the experience of the preservice teachers as well.

SHARED ACCOUNTABILITY AND THE IMPORTANCE OF COLLABORATION AND COMMUNICATION SKILLS

In each of the interviews, the teachers stressed that preservice students need to reconsider how they view teaching and collaboration. They want the preservice teachers to understand that the idea of a teacher in the same grade and even the same classroom for 30 or more years is a thing of the past. Like many education scholars and organizations, the teachers highlight that to meet the demands of teaching today, preservice teachers need opportunities to develop their collaborative skills while in their teacher preparation program (ATE, 2008; AACTE, 2010; Bullough et al., 2003; Darling-Hammond, 2006; Gardiner & Robinson, 2009; Grossman, 2010).

Furthermore, they feel preservice teachers should be aware of both the positive and negatives of shared accountability; and that, now more than ever, they need communication skills and the ability to compromise, for example, as Karyn points out:

> There needs to be some discussion with the students that there needs to be openness to the fact that things aren't always going to go their way. I think that is tricky in teaching because before we looked at it as a very isolated profession. This is my room these are my students, but that's not the reality of where education is going. And really kids benefit and teachers benefit when they open doors to collaboration. The onus is on the college students to be open and aware of the need to collaboration with whomever you get partnered with because you can't pick your colleagues. That is the reality.

The teachers explain that because their school is data driven, the administration moves people around as they see fit, sometimes taking into consideration preferences, but not always. Of the teachers interviewed, two of the teachers were a newly formed team in a collaborative classroom. Another just moved from 1st to K and another from K to 2nd. The teachers explained that sometimes teams work well, sometimes they don't. When it does work it is wonderful; however, when it doesn't work, they still have to come to work. They find a way to make the best of it. As Meredith describes:

> It is great when it does work and you do talk but it's hard when it's not best combination, as you have to come to work every day. What do you do to successfully get through those moments? It doesn't always work with different philosophies and working styles. Especially as a special education teacher you can be told "this is your space too, move in, use it how you need it, make it your home." In another room it's "here is your basket that is where your stuff can go."

Preservice teachers are often unprepared for this reality. They often enter the profession, assuming they will have choice in the grade they teach and imagine they will stay in the same grade for several years. Although they are aware of the many first-year challenges they will face such as learning the new curriculum, planning and teaching lessons for a full day every day, and class management issues, they often do not anticipate the workplace challenges of compromising with colleagues and may not have strategies for working closely with difficult people.

In the interviews, all of the teachers state that they are fortunate because they work in a school that values and supports their collaboration. The principal, a former teacher and graduate of our program, makes time for them to meet weekly in grade-level team meetings and professional learning communities. This time supports their success as it allows for teachers to learn from each other, share responsibilities, and collectively problem-solve (Dufour & Eaker, 1998). The teachers stressed the value of this time for planning and comparing how their lessons and units are going, for sharing resources, and for overall support.

In addition, the 2nd-grade teachers discussed the benefit of having time for collaboration around the relatively new expectations of analyzing and interpreting student data:

> We requested time to for looking at assessment and had a professional day and sat down together and calibrated our thinking. This is so important—things are getting harder to juggle and there is more to juggle. The need to calibrate thinking across grade level is critical especially with assessment. It effects and guides our instruction. . . . Your college students are coming in at time where everything is data driven if they don't know how to interpret data and use data to drive instruction the point is lost.

Collaboratively analyzing student data not only ensures consistency across the grade level, but it also provides opportunities for the teachers to discuss what their findings means for their instruction. Together, they look at each other's student work to problem-solve and help each other plan for ways to effectively differentiate their instruction.

To help prepare the preservice students they are mentoring for this type of collaboration, the teachers open their grade-level meetings so students can experience firsthand how grade-level collaboration looks and works, as Camille describes:

> If the partners come in and see that the teacher is partnering with their grade level colleagues they can see that even though we are different people, we work well and have goals, we respect each other and there is give and take in conversation with colleagues. The college students need to understand from very beginning that although there is an important accountability, and you have to

do your fair share of work, there still needs to be a give we are not coming to table with same set of strengths you have to accept that and you have to support each other.

To observe and participate in successful collaborative teams during their teacher preparation program is a powerful and invaluable learning experience for preservice teachers. Students in my seminar often share what they have learned at the meetings. The students who have been included in their teachers' collaborative planning have requested to work in grade-based groups to develop their own units.

BENEFITS OF TEACHER COLLABORATION WHEN WORKING WITH FAMILIES

In each of the interviews, the teachers noted that with all of the pressure put on them and all of things they have to do in a day, they simply couldn't do their jobs without the support of their colleagues. The teachers stressed the benefit of shared accountability and collaboration, in particular, when working with families. The author was surprised when the teachers talked about the changes they notice in the way parents speak to them and the increase in the general mistrust parents have in them. The teachers revealed that they feel less respected now than even just 5 years ago.

While numerous factors are certainly at work, the lack of trust isn't surprising given the intensity of the politicized criticism of the past few years. A famous *Time* magazine cover story framed most teachers as ineffective "rotten apples" that are impossible to remove from the classroom (Edwards, 2014). In New Jersey in particular, Governor Chris Christie is well known for his attacks on teachers and the teachers' union (Layton, 2015).

In the interviews, the teachers emphasized that preservice teachers should be prepared for working with parents in new ways. As one veteran teacher explains,

> It is important to help students understand that we live in a different culture of how parents view teachers with a lot of the political things that are happening and the impact that has on parents' ideas of what we are like before they even enter the classroom. I feel there are a lot of views out there that are being pushed that teachers are lazy, teachers don't care and that teachers are just there. I don't know where they are getting all the information, but they are getting that information and believing it. It may not be a personal attack, but it effects how they deal with us. There is not always a trust relationship and we are often not respected or treated as professionals. It is more "I have to tell you what you should be doing."

Janice, a teacher for over 20 years, compares her approach to parents to that of a small business owner:

> I think of it as owning my own business. They're my costumers. I have to speak with them and keep them though I have to be the expert too. I can't let them tell me what to do even though they think they know.

The teachers agreed that teacher collaboration, shared accountability, and the use of data-based evidence are crucial in handling parent mistrust. Analyzing student work together and sometimes having more than one teacher at parent–teacher conferences can be helpful to both seasoned and new teachers. Amy offers advice to novice teachers:

> The biggest thing is being able to back up what you're doing with parents—they are going to question what you think they would never question. You need to back it up and defend it. Be confident in yourself and find research to back it up, and data.

Of course, the ability to communicate with parents and withstand parental criticism can be difficult for new teachers who are often not prepared by their teacher education programs to deal with real families. In the college classroom we can role-play and provide simulations; however, much of this learning best happens in the schools under the mentorship of associated teacher educators.

SUMMING IT UP: LEARNING FROM VETERAN TEACHERS

Throughout the interviews, the teachers offered many valuable suggestions for teacher preparation programs:

- In addition to teaching content, pedagogy and instructional methods, programs should focus on developing communication and professional skills of preservice teachers (Gardiner, 2009; Lawley et al., 2014). This can be done through encouraging or requiring classes in public speaking and even acting or improvisation. Thinking of teacher as performer is not a new idea (see Sarason, 1999), but certainly one worth revisiting in teacher preparation programs.

    In addition, discussing and role-playing professional/workplace skills such as introducing themselves, assertiveness, and giving and taking feedback would help develop these "soft" skills.
- Although most teacher programs have students practice lessons in the college classroom, to assist students in learning how to manage flow and

timing of a lesson, teacher educators could include timed increments with distractions (phone ringing, mock fire drill) and give other students roles that they would find in the classroom (pencil player, meanderer, hungry student, etc.).
- To better prepare students for collaborative assessment, when looking at sample work and rubrics for analysis, preservice teachers should talk through and score work together to practice calibrating their thinking, and then discuss ways data can inform instruction. They can also role-play presenting data to others, such as parents.

Although the teachers provide useful suggestions for what university-based teacher educators can do in our courses, this chapter highlights the many aspects of teaching that can be learned in the field only under the mentorship of a classroom teacher. One thing that struck the author from the interviews is just how willing the teachers are to help. They all say that they wish they had more time with the students. They offered to come to campus to speak to the students there.

They asked if they can conduct a group seminar or panel at their school. They are unbelievably generous with their time and expertise. They enjoy having the students, and they are invested in developing future teachers, and they care. As Janice remarks, on her recent experience mentoring students: "I was so excited. They gave me a fresh view again of what I'm really here for with all rest of things going on. To see them so excited. I was like 'Wow! I remember feeling like that.'"

Some of this openness is no doubt due to the fact that they work in a school where they have support, resources, and time for planning. The school is located in a wealthy, high-performing district; the teachers are invested and successful "educative mentors" (Feiman-Nemser, 1998) working in a collaborative environment. However, even given all these factors, the author would have never realized how much they are willing to share until asked for their expertise from a position of trust and respect.

The ATE Standards for Field Experience in Teacher Education (2000) stress that clinical experience should be planned and deliberate, and collaboratively developed and implemented by both the institutions of higher education and the schools. However, the standards also note that these relationships take time. It is more common for large research-based universities to have well-developed and funded programs with strong ties between university and schools. As Ken Zeichner (2010) points out, it is important to find out how to build these relationships in all types of programs.

Teacher education program at small colleges often don't have access to lab schools, and the school–university relationships are built from the ground up. In the author's case, it took 5 years of working with the school before formally asking the teachers for their feedback on the teacher education program.

The teachers had many questions for the author about how the college program worked, what was discussed in the seminar, how the student partners were paired. Although we had meetings where the author gave an overview of the program and their role, she never opened the door for collaborative reflection on the program as a whole and how best to prepare teachers. This important (yet somewhat obvious in retrospect) realization will hopefully lead to more open and honest communication in the future and deepen our institutional ties.

Finally, the author was somewhat surprised and disappointed when one of the teachers commented that sometimes new teachers come into the field with a negative attitude toward more experienced teachers; that they sometimes assume the stereotype that veterans are not up on the latest methods or technology or just don't care anymore. While this may be true in some cases, it is important, now more than ever, to appreciate the wisdom and experience of veteran teachers, just as they appreciate new teachers. As one teacher remarks,

> If we want to be as effective as we possibly can and achieve the incredible amount that we have to achieve then we need each other. We have to help each other. If you don't you are making it the hardest job ever.

Mutual respect and collaboration between university-based teacher educators and associated teacher educators leads to better learning environments and outcomes for preservice teachers. As they told me at the end of the interview, "sharing is caring."

REFERENCES

American Association of Colleges for Teacher Education. (2010). *The clinical preparation of teachers: A policy brief.* Washington, DC: Author. Retrieved from https://aacte.org/pdf/Government_Relations/Clinical%20Prep%20Paper_03-11-2010.pdf

Ammentorp, L., & Madden, L. (2014) Partnered placements: Creating and supporting successful collaboration among preservice teachers. *Journal of Early Childhood Teacher Education, 35*(2), 135–149.

Ammentorp, L. & Madden, L. (in press). Maximizing successful collaboration between pre-service teachers. *The Educational Forum.*

Association of Teacher Educators (ATE). (2008). *Standards for teacher educators.* Retrieved from http://www.ate1.org/pubs/uploads/tchredstds0308.pdf

Association of Teacher Educators (ATE), Commission on Classroom Teachers as Associated Teacher Educators. (n.d). Retrieved from http://ateprofdev.com/

Association of Teacher Educators (ATE), Task Force on Field Experience Standards. (2000). *Standards for field experiences in teacher education*. Reston, VA. Retrieved from http://www.ate1.org/pubs/uploads/nfdfstds.pdf

Bullough, R. V., Jr. (2005). Being and becoming a mentor: School-based teacher educators and teacher educator identity. *Teaching and Teacher Education, 21*(2), 143–155.

Bullough, R. V., Jr., Young, J., Erickson, L., Birrell, J. R., Clark, D. C., & Egan, M. W. (2003). Teaching with a peer: A comparison of two models of student teaching. *Teaching and Teacher Education, 19*, 57–73. doi: 10.1016/S0742–051X(02)00094-X

Darling-Hammond, L. (2006). Constructing 21st-century teacher education. *Journal of Teacher Education, 57*(3), 300–314.

Darling-Hammond, L., Hammerness, K., Grossman, P., Rust, F., & Shulman, L. (2005). The design of teacher education programs. In L. Darling-Hammond & J. Bransford (Eds.), *Preparing teachers for a changing world* (pp. 390–441). San Francisco, CA: Jossey Bass.

DuFour, R., & Eaker, R. (1998). *Professional learning communities at work: Best practices for enhancing student achievement*. Bloomington, IN: National Educational Service.

Edwards, H. S. (2014, November). The war on teacher tenure. *Time*. Retrieved from http://time.com/magazine/

Feiman-Nemser, S. (1998). Teachers as teacher educators. *European Journal of Teacher Education in Europe, 21*(1), 63–74.

Feiman-Nemser, S. (2001). From preparation to practice: Designing a continuum to strengthen and sustain teaching. *Teachers College Record, 103*(6), 1013–1055.

Feiman-Nemser, S., & Beasley, K. (2007). Discovering and sharing knowledge: Inventing a new role for cooperating teachers. In D. Carroll, H. Featherstone, J. Featherstone, S. Feiman-Nemser, & D. Roosevelt (Eds.), *Transforming teacher education: Reflections from the field* (pp. 139–160). Cambridge, MA: Harvard Education Press.

Feiman-Nemser, S., & Buchmann, M. (1985). Pitfalls of experience in teacher education. *Teachers College Record, 87*, 49–65.

Gardiner, W. (2009). Rudderless as mentors: The challenge of teachers as mentors. *Action in Teacher Education, 30*(4), 56–66.

Gardiner, W., & Robinson, K. (2009). Paired field placements: A means for collaboration. *The New Educator, 5*:81–94.

Grossman, P. (2010). *Learning to practice: The design of clinical experience in teacher preparation*. Policy Brief of the partnership for Teacher Quality. Washington, DC: American Association of the Colleges for Teacher Education.

Hargreaves, A., & Fullan, M. (2012). *Professional capital: Transforming teaching in every school*. New York, NY: Teachers College Press.

Lawley, J. J., Moore, J., & Smajic, A. (2014). Effective communication between preservice and cooperating teachers. *The New Educator, 10*(2), 153–162.

Layton, L. (2015, August 3). Chris Christie to teachers union: You deserve a punch in the face. *The Washington Post*. Retrieved from: https://www.washingtonpost.com

Leana, C.R. (2011, Fall). The missing link in school reform. *Stanford Social Innovation Review*, *9*(4), 34.

National Council for Accreditation of Teacher Education. (2010). *Transforming teacher education through clinical practice: A national strategy to prepare effective teachers*. Washington, DC: Report of the Blue Ribbon Panel on Clinical Preparation and Partnerships for Improved Student Learning. Retrieved from http://www.ncate.org/LinkClick.aspx?fileticket=zzeiB1OoqPk%3D&tabid=715

Sarason, S. (1999). *Teaching as a performing art*. New York, NY: Teacher's College Press.

Torrez, C.A.F., & Krebs, M. M. (2012). Expert voices: What cooperating teachers and teacher candidates say about quality student teaching placements and experiences, *Action in Teacher Education, 34*(5–6), 485–499.

Young, J. R., Bullough., R. V., Jr., Draper, R. J., Smith, L. K., & Erickson, L. B. (2005). Novice teacher growth and personal models of mentoring: Choosing compassion over inquiry. *Mentoring and Tutoring, 13*(2), 169–188.

Zeichner K. (2010). Rethinking the connections between campus courses and field experiences in college-and university-based teacher education, *Journal of Teacher Education, 61* (1), 89–99.

Zeichner, K., & Liston, D. (2014). *Reflective teaching: An introduction* (2nd ed.). New York, NY: Routledge.

Chapter 5

Classroom Teachers as Associate Teacher Educator Perspectives

Framing Dialogues and Professional Development Contexts among Professional Educators

Caroline M. Crawford

ABSTRACT

The focus of this effort was to develop a more fully developed understanding of the areas of necessity and desired areas of further understanding among novice and veteran classroom teachers. Classroom teachers who also engage in the vitally important roles of field-based associate teacher educators are constantly giving of themselves toward others in the field of teacher education. An interesting thought, however, is that classroom teachers may rarely have opportunities to share their own insights revolving around the teacher education process.

To address this concern, a case study based approach has resulted in the recognition of inherent responses by the silent majority of classroom teachers, and especially classroom teachers who hold the dual roles of associate teacher educators. This discussion presents the areas of professional development need among novice and veteran classroom teachers.

KEYWORDS

classroom teachers, novice classroom educators, teacher candidates, teacher leader, teaching and learning, university supervisors, veteran classroom teacher educators

BACKGROUND

One of the initial areas of focus within the Association of Teacher Educators' (ATE) Commission on Classroom Teachers as Associated Teacher Educators has been to learn more about areas that require or may desire supportive documentation and perhaps online professional development opportunities. The initial framework for the Commission discussion focused upon *Teaching and Learning*, as well as the following two questions: What would classroom teachers want university supervisors to know? and, What would classroom teachers want novice classroom educators to know?

After an extensive discussion during the February 2014 Commission meeting, the Commission extended the areas of focus to include: What are your thoughts about teaching and learning as a whole?; What would classroom teachers want university supervisors to know?; What would classroom teachers want novice classroom educators to know?; What would novice classroom teachers want veteran classroom teacher educators to know?; and, What are important qualities/components of teacher leader that are necessary to support novice teachers?

The Commission delved into the teaching and learning topic, resulting in seven thematic areas of focus: teaching support, instructional design, teaching experience, philosophical beliefs systems, subject matter expertise, professional community of learners and of practice, and types of learning environments. These areas of emphasis were realized as significant and appropriate toward supporting the cognitive frameworks of understanding and professional areas of expertise as understood by the classroom teachers.

COMMUNITIES OF PRACTICE FRAMEWORK

Learning communities is an umbrella approach toward understanding relationships, connectedness, and social senses of positive vulnerability and support that occurs within different social groups of people who come together toward reaching a specific goal or achievement. Several years ago, Wenger (1998, 2009) delved into communities of practice as more professional realms of social engagement and understanding, suggesting that people choose to come together for specific periods of time and toward reaching very specific levels of success.

This may be toward learning new information or coming together toward achieving a goal, but with the focus being within a professional understanding of knowledge engagement and dispositional success. A well-known question as offered by Wenger (1998) is stated, "So, what if we adopted a different perspective, one that placed learning in the context of our lived experience of participation in the world?" (p. 3; Wenger, 2009, p. 210). This question recognized the needs to engage within a more real-world participatory experience within one's real world environments.

This recognition led toward practical realms of engagement as field-based areas of consideration that nicely parallels a metaphoric framework of understanding designated as a landscape or field. An interesting *next step* approach to the concept of communities of practice was recognized by Wenger-Trayner, Fenton-O'Creevy, Hutchinson, Kubiak, and Wenger-Trayner (2015) as learning in landscapes of practice that fulfilled a greater understanding associated with professional communities. This brilliantly framed the efforts of teacher preparation programs and the teacher education profession as a whole.

PURPOSE

The purpose of this intrinsic case study approach was to further understand classroom teacher's beliefs, opinions, and experiences as regards their roles as associated teacher educators, specifically, to develop a more fully developed understanding of the areas of necessity and desired areas of further understanding among novice and veteran classroom teachers.

The Commission recognized the need to enhance the dialogue that currently occurs among classroom teachers, toward developing a more holistic approach toward perceptions, understandings and differentiations in approach that may be recognized within many teacher education programs of study.

SIGNIFICANCE

Recognizing the transformational impact that classroom teachers have upon the teacher education process, it is vitally important to obtain the input pertaining to strengths, weaknesses, and areas of further engagement consideration as framed through classroom teachers. The overarching results of this approach reflect significant themes and subthemes that were highlighted.

STANDARDS FOR TEACHER EDUCATORS

The Association of Teacher Educators' Standards for Teacher Educators (ATE, n.d.) reflect upon the dispositional levels of engagement, understanding, and indicators that more fully embrace the realm of teacher educators. Throughout this initial foray into the presentation of burgeoning themes and subthemes that arose from this qualitative analysis of the data, the manuscript embeds an understanding of the following nine standards:

- STANDARD 1 Teaching;
- STANDARD 2 Cultural Competence;
- STANDARD 3 Scholarship;
- STANDARD 4 Professional Development;
- STANDARD 5 Program Development;
- STANDARD 6 Collaboration;
- STANDARD 7 Public Advocacy;
- STANDARD 8 Teacher Education Profession; and,
- STANDARD 9 Vision (Association of Teacher Educators, n.d., pp. 1–8).

RESEARCH QUESTION

As the purpose of the study was to further understand classroom teacher's beliefs, opinions, and experiences as regards their roles as associated teacher educators, the research question of inquiry was designated as: How do novice and veteran teacher educators view the teacher education program engagement and dialogic understanding in the teaching and learning process that occurs within schools?

FRAMING THE ENVIRONMENT AND METHODOLOGICAL APPROACH

This study was embedded within two large school districts that are located in the suburban communities that surround a large metropolitan area in the southern United States of America. The classroom educators asked to respond to the designated open-ended questions:

- What are your thoughts about teaching and learning as a whole?
- What would classroom teachers want university supervisors to know?
- What would classroom teachers want novice classroom educators to know?
- What would novice classroom teachers want veteran classroom teacher educators to know?
- What are important qualities/components of teacher leader that are necessary to support novice teachers?

As an intrinsic case study methodological approach, the focus of this effort is interesting due to its ordinary expectation of discursive engagement that professionals would normally engage in and recognize as imperative, necessary levels of discourse and to better understand what classroom teachers reflect upon when asked to focus upon the designated questions (Stake, 1995, 2005).

Participants

The participants were asked to respond to these questions during their regular workday hours, in casual discussion environments toward achieving a comfortableness and sense of thoughtful approach that would reflect an *off the top of my head* response approach. The desire was to lessen the effort toward responding in a politically correct manner, and to achieve responses that were not carefully framed and censored. For this reason, anonymity was an extremely important aspect of this qualitative engagement.

PROCEDURES

The questionnaire was implemented as an informal initial survey of classroom teachers so as to more fully develop an understanding of the areas of necessity and desired areas of further understanding among novice and veteran classroom teachers. The informal survey results reflect classroom teachers, both novice and veteran, within the range of the K-12 instructional environments. Also included in discussions were student teaching teacher candidates, so as to ensure that a fully articulated understanding of the teacher candidate needs was framed.

DATA ANALYSIS

The data were analyzed implementing the grounded theory approach, focused upon identifying naturally developing patterns and themes throughout the data (Charmaz, 2003, 2014; Creswell, 2007). The grounded theory approach emphasizes the theoretical structure that is developed as grounded within the data and is understood through the thematic outcomes that engage in the process that is supported by the participant data.

The coding occurred by hand, with overarching themes and subthemes being the clarified articulations of understanding as emphasized by the data sets. A constant comparative analytical method (Glaser & Strauss, 1967) supported the coding effort, emphasizing connectedness and insight throughout the data sets.

FINDINGS

The results of the informal survey of classroom teachers, as well as delving into research on the subject matter resulted in the following areas of thematic and subthematic focus as framed through the primary questions.

What Are Your Thoughts About Teaching and Learning as a Whole?

The primary themes that arose within the teaching and learning realm include the following: teaching support, instructional design, teaching experience, philosophical beliefs systems, subject matter expertise, professional community of learners and of practice, and types of learning environments. These primary themes were intriguing due to the clearly articulated focus of classroom teachers upon major research areas. To more clearly reflect the subthemes highlighted by the data analysis, the themes are designated in Table 5.1.

Table 5.1 *Teaching and Learning Themes*

Theme	Subtheme	Level Three Theme
Teaching support	Mentoring	Formal mentoring
		Informal mentoring
	Teaching support	Formal teaching support
		Informal teaching support
Instructional design	Technology	Learners
	Syllabus	Self
	Analysis	Colleagues
	Instructional goals and objectives	
	Assessments	
Teaching experience	Prior experience	
	Formal teaching	
	Informal teaching	
Philosophical belief systems	Learning theories	Formal
	Reflective practices	Informal
	Self-study	
	Student evaluations	
Subject matter expertise	Motivation	
Professional community of learners and of practice	Engagement	
	Clarity	
	"Presence"	
Types of learning environs	Face-to-face	
	Online	
	Blended/hybrid	
	Field-based	

The classroom teachers expressed thoughts surrounding teaching and learning as areas of importance and direct impact upon the profession, and especially upon classroom teachers as associated teacher educators, are integrally impacted.

What Would Classroom Teachers Want University Supervisors to Know?

The primary themes that arose within the question revolving around what classroom teachers would want university supervisors to know were intriguing. The primary themes are presented as follows:

- How to supervise a student teacher; classroom assessments;
- What is response to intervention (RTI)? (in reality, not just in theory);
- Classroom management;
- Technological competence;
- Cultural competence diversity;
- Building district hierarchies and curriculum hierarchies;
- Disposition;
- Theory versus reality; and,
- Teaching as a profession.

These primary themes were intriguing, with a more fully developed representation of the articulated subthemes highlighted by the data analysis, represented in Table 5.2.

The extensive feedback and thematic areas of emphasis are significant and worthy of consideration and discourse at a more detailed level of engagement.

What Would Classroom Teachers Want Novice Classroom Educators to Know?

The primary themes that arose within the question revolving around what classroom teachers would want novice classroom educators to know were also intriguing. Novice classroom educators are designated as teacher candidates and early career classroom teachers. The primary themes included the following:

- Establishing a means of communication from day one;
- Basic differentiation strategies;
- "Go to's";
- Management; assessments; relationships with other teachers;
- Small groups;

Table 5.2 Classroom Teacher Guidance to University Supervisors

Theme	Subtheme	Level Three Theme
How to supervise a student teacher	Observations	Require frequent visits
		Require immediate feedback
		Focus upon lesson planning
		Focus upon classroom management
		Analyze impact upon student learning
	Lesson plans	Nothing like what is taught in school
		Lengthy plans to think through lesson cycle
	Initial classroom and student assessment	Know type of students you are getting
		Maintain engaged, attentive, study habits
		Students eager to learn at a higher level
	Management	
	Time	
	Qualifications	
	Communications	
	Know teacher candidates	Work ethic
		Knowledge of subject
		Understand concepts and theories
		Impact factor: single parent
		Impact factor: outside job
	Student teach in fall	Set up classroom
		Establish discipline
		Build relationship with student and parent
Classroom assessments	Formative vs. summative	
What is response to intervention (RTI)? (in reality, not just in theory)	Formal vs. informal	
	What does it look like	
	How is it organized	
	Data	What information is used
		How long should we track students
Classroom management		
Technological competence	Can't use software/tools	
	Technology regulations	District technology regulations
		School site technology regulations
	Model incorporating tech	Teacher-centered
		Student-centered
Cultural competence diversity	White privilege	
	Generalizations	

Theme	Subtheme	Level Three Theme
	Awareness of	Thoughts
		Words
		Actions
	How to teach individuals	Severe behavior problems
		Lazy
		Special needs
	Diverse learners	Operating as problem solvers
		Take advantage of student strengths:
		• felicity with technology
		• fluent communication
		• interpersonal negotiation
		• use of every hour of every day
		Different learning styles
		Students need more guidance, are not:
		• self-regulated
		• independent
		• personally motivated
		Are not "linear anchors"
Building district hierarchies and curriculum hierarchies	Realities of buildings	
	Politics	
	Grade-level curriculum awareness	
	Scope and sequence	
	Pacing guides	
	Pacing in general	
	Day-to-day activities	
	Culture of the campus	
	Opportunities to improve grades	
Disposition	Watch your	Attitude
		Facial expressions
		Verbal language
		Body language
	Self-regulation	
	Patience	
	Self-efficacy	
	Self-control	
	Communication	
Theory versus reality	Use real-life examples	How to manage them
	Classrooms are not utopia	Struggles in all children
		Disabilities in all children
	Real interactions	With real children/students
		Work in small groups of students
		Different grade levels

(Continued)

Table 5.2 (Continued)

Theme	Subtheme	Level Three Theme
	Ideal picture of teaching	Real-life situations may not match up
		Being flexible is a must
		Know the student and the subject
		Hard but rewarding field
Teaching as a profession	Salary schedule	
	Insured	
	National Education Association	
	Kappa Delta Pi	
	Budgets	School budgets
		District budgets
		Technology budgets
	District vs. district	Differences between district expectations
		Performance ratings
		Boundary lines for schools (zoning)
	Taxes	

- Time management; disposition;
- Teaching as a profession; and,
- Teaching as a reality.

These primary themes were intriguing, with a more fully developed representation of the articulated subthemes highlighted by the data analysis, represented in Table 5.3.

The extensive feedback and thematic areas of emphasis are significant and worthy of consideration and discourse at a more detailed level of engagement, not only among classroom teachers and novice classroom teachers, but also within a triad-focused transformational approach that embeds communications between classroom teachers and university supervisors, as well as novice classroom educators and university supervisors.

What Would Novice Classroom Teachers Want Veteran Classroom Teacher Educators to Know?

The primary themes that arose within the question revolving around what novice classroom teachers would want veteran classroom educators to know were also intriguing. The primary themes included the following: qualifications; salary; attitude; technology; renewal; focus; collaboration; and, leadership. These primary themes were intriguing, with a more fully developed

Table 5.3 Classroom Teachers Guidance to Novice Classroom Educators

Theme	Subtheme	Level Three Theme
Establishing a means of communication From day one: Relationships with parents	Means of communication	Phone Personal E-mail Blog Website
	Conferences	How often to have them How to document them What evidence is needed How to express a negative in a positive way Dress code Professionalism
Basic differentiation strategies	Theory/research vs reality What it looks and sounds like Tools used Different group levels Small groups	
	Modifying lessons	Adaptability
	Student discussion	Powerful tool
	Learn to find information	Apply what they learn
"Go to's"	Books	PD in library
	Partners/mentors on campus Pinterest Teacher blogs Management plan Community builders Content practice guides	
	Higher-level thinking	Drive instruction Drive discussions
	Technology	Training on basic use and integration Online professional development Engaging for students
Management	Have a plan Maintain high expectations Front load Be consistent Gradual release Positive reinforcement	Practice in the beginning of the year
	Classroom management	Don't be afraid to discipline Be easy on yourself Double intensity your first year
	Key to success	Be consistent Always fair

(Continued)

Table 5.3 (Continued)

Theme	Subtheme	Level Three Theme
Assessment	How/what to assess	
	Informal	Small groups
		Anecdotal notes
	Formal	End of unit test
		DCA
		STAAR
Relationships with other teachers	Don't burn bridges	
	Learn from others	But make it your own
	Aware of surroundings	Never put down peers or district in public
	Be a team player	
	Be helpful	
	Observe	
	Collaborate	
	Share	
Small groups	Do them!	Can be as simple as working with a table
	Keep notes	
	Be consistent	
	Focus on bubble kiddos	
	Have a plan	
Time management	Be realistic	Don't try to be an expert at everything
		Don't' reinvent the wheel
	Set goals	Focus on 1–2 goals per year
	Partition	Focus on work at work
		Take time for yourself
		Come early or stay late, don't do both!
Disposition	Watch your	Attitude
		Facial expressions
		Verbal language
		Body language
	Self-regulation	
	Self-awareness	
	Emotional investment	Show that you care about the students
		You care about what they're interested in
	Positive	Don't let others taint your vision
	Take risks	
	Ability to deal with distractions	

Theme	Subtheme	Level Three Theme
Teaching as a profession	Unions	Reasons both for and against joining
		Differences between them
	Reimbursements	
	Salary schedule	
	Insurance	
	Mental health days	Take a break
Teaching as a reality	Real world vs college	What you learn in college does not prepare
		Be prepared, teaching is not easy
		Requires a lot of time
		A lot of work
		Patience with students and oneself
		Lesson plans will most likely change:
		• this is normal • one should adjust and be flexible
	It's OK to be stressed	It's OK to feel like you're failing
	First year can be overwhelming	
	Know the content	
	Establish rapport with students	
	Efficient with admin. Functions	
	Gets better with experience	
	First 3 years are trial and error	
	Mental and physical strain	
	Be organized!	
	Be passionate for students	

representation of the articulated subthemes highlighted by the data analysis, represented in Table 5.4.

The extensive feedback and thematic areas of emphasis are significant and worthy of consideration and discourse at a more detailed level of engagement, not only between novice classroom teachers and veteran classroom teachers as associated teacher educators, but with special discursive engagement between university supervisors and veteran classroom teachers as associated teacher educators.

What Are Important Qualities/Components of Teacher Leader That Are Necessary to Support Novice Teachers?

The primary themes that arose within the question revolving around what are the important qualities and components of teacher leaders that are necessary

Table 5.4 *Novice Classroom Teachers Want Veteran Classroom Teachers to Know*

Theme	Subtheme	Level Three Theme
Qualifications	Certified	
Salary	Raises	Determined by years of service
		Determined by what we bring in
	Entitled	Expect more but may not deserve it
Attitude	Respect	Novice teachers desire respect
	Listen and learn from older teachers	
	Veteran teachers are best resources	
	Need input	Intimidated and overwhelmed
	Compassionate	
	Want advice	
	Need advice	
	Excited and motivated	
	Have something to offer	
	Be open to new ideas	
	Ask a lot of questions	
	Need a lot of support	
	Need others to be patient	
	Need communication	
	New generations	Not worse than older generations
	Important: feel heard	Nice to receive credit for doing well
		Nobody wants to feel invisible
	Eager to learn	Afraid to bother veteran teachers
	Know content	But may struggle with process
	Sense of perspective	Expectations of first-year teachers
Technology	Integrating technology	
	Professional development	Training on different platforms
		Basic use
	Web 2.0 tools	
	Renewal/renewed	New ideas
		Energetic
		Optimistic
		Innovative
		Doing things differently isn't wrong
		Change can be good
		Novice want to learn from veterans
Focus	Instruction	More data driven
		More substance
	Performance	
	Building better people	
	Scores matter	
	College readiness	
	Teaching strategies	As times change, so does teaching
		Instructional technologies
		Interaction
		Flexibility

Theme	Subtheme	Level Three Theme
Collaboration	Novice teachers need help	
	Open to mix ideas	Past/present
	Need support	
	Time	To "get it together"
		Takes novice teachers longer
		Apologize for all the questions
		Time and knowledge is appreciated
Leadership	Role-models	
	Experts	

to support novice teachers were especially intriguing. It is important to note that teacher leaders were defined by the participants as mentor teachers, classroom-based supervisors, and field-based supervisors. The primary themes included the following:

- Disposition;
- Knowledgeable;
- Qualifications;
- Self-awareness;
- Collaboration;
- Role model; and,
- Relational.

These primary themes were intriguing, with a more fully developed representation of the articulated subthemes highlighted by the data analysis, represented in Table 5.5.

The extensive feedback and thematic areas of emphasis are significant and worthy of consideration and discourse at a more detailed level of engagement, within all levels of teacher education discourse. Teacher leaders are not only framed as classroom teachers or as university supervisors, but burgeoning teacher leaders must also be supported, recognized, and embraced as the next wave of teacher education's leadership.

LIMITATIONS

There are limitations associated with this study. First is the recognized difficulty associated with the establishment of the finding's reliability and validity. The analysis of the data through a constant comparative method may reflect the researcher's understandings of the field and discursive read of the text through a potentially differentiated social lens of understanding. Finally,

Table 5.5 *Qualities/Components of Teacher Leaders: Necessary to Support Novice Classroom Teachers*

Theme	Subtheme	Level Three Theme
Disposition	Approachable	
	Realistic	
	Consistent	
	Positive	
	Patient	
	Time management	Punctual
	Helpful	
	Honest	
	Kind	
	Sense of humor	
	Energetic	
	Motivating	
	Dedicated	
	Invested	
	Organized	
	Optimistic attitude	
	Passionate	About teaching
		About helping students
	Communicates often	
	Communication skills	
	Confidence in content area	
	Commitment to lead by example	
	Creative ability	Address learning styles/needs
	Inspirational	
	Compassionate	
	Responsible	
	Organized	
	Friendly	
	Empathetic (empathy)	
	Good listener	
	Encouraging	
	Honest	
	Real-world experience	
	Encourage learning	
	Supportive	
	Approachable	
	Experienced	
	Availability	Regular meetings held
		Appointments are kept
		Dedicate time
Knowledgeable	Content	
	Policies	
	Procedures	School operations
	Strategies	
	Technology integration	

Theme	Subtheme	Level Three Theme
	Curriculum	
	Pacing	
	Classroom management strategies	
	Provide admin. support	
	School expectations	Written
		Unwritten
Qualifications	Years of service	
	Degree	
	Student performance	
	PDAS ranking	
Self-awareness	Strengths	
	Potential limitations	
	Critical of self	
	Willing to learn	
	Admit fault	
Collaboration	Willing to share	
	Share materials	
	Templates	
	Exchange ideas	
Role model	In the classroom	Caring about students and teachers
		Concerned about good education
		Desire to see students succeed
		Willing to work with students
	Outside the classroom	Collegial
		Professional
		Stay away from gossip
	Stay away from negativity	Erode relationships with
		• Fellow teachers
		• Parents
		• Students
		• Administration
Relational	Understanding	
	Remember when you were new	
	Feelings of being overwhelmed	
	Feelings of being stressed	
	Share experiences	
	Share instructional materials	
	Patient answering questions	
	Give constructive criticism	
	Listen more than speak	
	Build on strengths	Rather than eliminate weaknesses
	Need to feel heard and appreciated	
	Feel valued	
	Offers help and advice	Frequently and as desired

the qualitative nature of the study reflects a difficulty toward implementing the findings beyond the specific scope of this study effort. The relevance and practical understanding of the findings may not extend beyond this specific intrinsic case study.

CONCLUSION

The findings of this study reflect a discourse and community of engagement that embraces a social relevance and professional relevance that emphasizes the depth and breadth of the professional education field. The shifting landscape of the professional education field, including within this discussion is the teacher education and preparation programs, recognize the relationships that are inherent toward successfully engaging in transformational journeys for teacher candidates, novice classroom teachers, veteran classroom teachers as associated teacher educators, and university supervisors.

Through a focused approach upon learning in landscapes of practice (Wenger-Trayner et al., 2015), the grounding of the profession may be more fully realized. With the initial efforts of the Commission, a developing Annotated Bibliography supports a developing understanding of the research in the field which is integrally important toward framing the discussion.

However, of vital importance is ensuring that the voices of classroom teachers, novice and veteran classroom teachers, are represented. This chapter presents the areas of professional development need among novice and veteran classroom teachers, with the focused effort being an understanding of classroom teachers through their own input.

ACKNOWLEDGMENTS

Special appreciation is offered toward the contributors, without whom this endeavor would have been significantly more difficult. I offer my sincere appreciation for the professional expertise and efforts of Julie Blackmer Desselles and Jennifer Nguyen.

REFERENCES

Association of Teacher Educators (ATE). (n.d.). *Standards for Teacher Educators*. Retrieved from http://www.ate1.org/pubs/uploads/tchredstds0308.pdf

Charmaz, K. (2003). Grounded theory—objectivist and constructivist methods. In N. K. Denzin & Y. S. Lincoln (Eds.), *Strategies of qualitative inquiry* (pp. 249–291). London: Sage

Charmaz, K. (2014). *Constructing grounded theory.* Thousand Oaks, CA: SAGE Publications Ltd.

Creswell, J. W. (2007). *Qualitative inquiry and research design: Choosing among five traditions* (2nd ed.). Thousand Oaks, CA: Sage Publications.

Glaser, B. G., & Strauss, A. L. (1967). *The discovery of grounded theory: Strategies for qualitative research.* New York, NY: Aldine De Gruyter.

Stake, R. E. (1995). *The art of case study research.* Thousand Oaks, CA: Sage.

Stake, R. E. (2005). Qualitative case studies. In N. K. Denzin & Y. S. Lincoln (Eds.), *The Sage handbook of qualitative research* (3rd ed., pp. 443–466). Thousand Oaks, CA: Sage.

Wenger, E. (1998). *Communities of practice: Learning, meaning, and identity.* Cambridge, MA: Harvard University Press.

Wenger, E. (2009). A social theory of learning. In K. Illeris (Ed.), *Contemporary theories of learning: Learning theorists . . . in their own words.* New York, NY: Routledge.

Wenger-Trayner, E., Fenton-O'Creevy, M., Hutchinson, S., Kubiak, C., & Wenger-Trayner, B. (2015). *Learning in landscapes of practice: Boundaries, identify, and knowledgeability in practice-based learning.* New York, NY: Routledge.

Afterword

Caroline M. Crawford and Sandra L. Hardy

Through this text, the Association of Teacher Educators (ATE) and the ATE Commission on Classroom Teachers as Associated Teacher Educators have attempted to engage in a vital discussion that revolves around the integral importance of redefining teacher preparation and learning from experience in the development of classroom teachers as associated teacher educators. The three separate yet related texts of focus are designated as:

- *Redefining Teacher Preparation: Learning From Experience in Educator Development*
- *Dynamic Principles of Professional Development: Essential Elements of Effective Teacher Preparation*
- *Teacher to Teacher Mentality: Purposeful Practice in Teacher Education*

This text came into being due to the vision of Nancy P. Gallavan, ATE president 2013–2014, who appointed this Commission and engaged Caroline M. Crawford as the Commission chairperson for a 3-year period.

Caroline articulated the Commission vision as moving toward redefining teacher preparation through learning from experience pertaining to advocacy, equity, leadership, and professionalism for classroom teachers as associated teacher educators in all settings.

Furthermore, this vision supports quality education and collegial collaboration for all learners. Further, the Commission's mission was expressed as the promotion of quality teacher education through exemplary collaborations and collegial understandings that reflect the inherent importance of classroom teachers as associated teacher educators.

Based upon the vision, mission, and goals of the Commission's efforts, this text is meant as a *state of the profession* as it revolves around the concept of redefining teacher education through learning through experience in the development of classroom teachers as associated teacher educators. This is an integrally important discussion to hold, and equally important to bring forward research and scholarly efforts toward more fully understanding and articulating the reciprocity that inherently occurs within the deep-seated cooperative relationships transpiring within the realms of teacher education.

This relationship emerges between teacher preparation programs, to professional educators within the school sites, to the teacher candidate who works with professional educators throughout the transformational journey into a student teacher and then into a novice classroom teacher. Yet within these cooperative relationships one is becoming more aware of and recognizes the deeply appreciated works of the classroom teacher who takes on significant additional mentorship and collegial professional development efforts as an associated teacher educator.

This text and the related books are an initial attempt to highlight the current understandings and associated scholarly efforts pertaining to each theme revolving around the important role of classroom teachers as associated teacher educators.

As a historical context toward framing the place of this text, and the other two sister publications, within the teacher education professional realm, classroom teachers have recognized their roles as a multifaceted approach toward the profession. Classroom teachers have been reinventing themselves, to fit within the Information Age and toward taking on differentiated roles that may be dependent upon differentiated learning theories of behaviorism, cognitivism, constructivism, and even connectivism, from *sage on the stage* to *facilitator* to *learner colleague* and beyond, dependent upon the instructional goals and instructional objectives.

A fun fact is that everyone has an opinion of the classroom teacher roles, including how classroom teachers should act, how classroom teachers should work, and even the different types of face-to-face, blended, and online learning environments in which classroom teachers currently find themselves engaged. Harrison and Killion (2007) stated that there are 10 roles for classroom teachers who are also actively engaged as teacher leaders, stated as being: "Resource Provider; Instructional Specialist; Curriculum Specialist; Classroom Supporter; Learning Facilitator; Mentor; School Leader; Data Coach; Catalyst for Change; and, Learner" (para. 3–21).

The Eton Institute also listed teacher roles that are inherently viable and useful within the 21st century: "The Controller; The Prompter; The Resource; The Assessor; The Organizer; The Participant; and, The Tutor" (n.d., para. 4–16). There are also innumerable researchers who desire to work out the beliefs, reasoning, and abilities of classroom teachers (Darling-Hammond,

2006; Kim, Kim, Lee, Spector, & DeMeester, 2013; Kleickmann et al., 2013; Nespor, 1987; Pajares, 1992; Putnam & Borko, 2000; Russell & Korthagen, 2013).

Yet after the researchers and scholars retreat to their offices with intriguing data sets and to work more closely with teacher candidates toward strengthening the candidate's understandings prior to the field-based experiences, a recognition arises. The depth of respect for classroom teachers as associated teacher educators undergirds an important recognition of the integral and reciprocal relationships felt by all professional educators.

The identity, pedagogy, and self-efficacy embedded within the education profession is more fully realized throughout the teacher education profession due to the synchronous dance that occurs between pedagogy and andragogy, self-efficacy and mentorship that embraces modeling, and transformational journeys that directly impact one's shifting identity and sense of self no matter whether as a developing teacher educator or a burgeoning teacher leader.

REFERENCES

Darling-Hammond, L. (2006). *Powerful teacher education: Lessons from exemplary programs*. San Francisco, CA: John Wiley & Sons.

Eton Institute (n.d.). *The 7 Roles of a Teacher in the 21st Century*. Retrieved from http://etoninstitute.com/blog/teacher-training/the-7-roles-of-a-teacher-in-the-21st-century

Harrison, C., & Killion, J. (2007, September). Ten roles for teacher leaders. *Educational Leadership, 65*(1), 74–77. Retrieved from http://tinyurl.com/6xf4tpq

Kim, C., Kim, M. K., Lee, C., Spector, J. M., & DeMeester, K. (2013). Teacher beliefs and technology integration. *Teaching and Teacher Education, 29*, 76–85. Retrieved from http://media.dropr.com/pdf/WEvqzmQRL2n2yxgXHBVTGHG G0tLjpzc1.pdf

Kleickmann, T., Richter, D., Kunter, M., Elsner, J., Besser, M., Krauss, S., & Baumert, J. (2013). Teachers' content knowledge and pedagogical content knowledge the role of structural differences in teacher education. *Journal of Teacher Education, 64*(1), 90–106. doi: 10.1177/0022487112460398 Retrieved from http://tinyurl.com/j557qds

Nespor, J. (1987). The role of beliefs in the practice of teaching. *Journal of Curriculum Studies, 19*(4), 317–328. Retrieved from http://files.eric.ed.gov/fulltext/ED270446.pdf

Pajares, M. F. (1992). Teachers' beliefs and educational research: Cleaning up a messy construct. *Review of Educational Research, 62*(3), 307–332. Retrieved from http://media.dropr.com/pdf/9gnziXcoKpR4NEygcZferbvB3HonvxCa.pdf

Putnam, R. T., & Borko, H. (2000). What do new views of knowledge and thinking have to say about research on teacher learning? *Educational Researcher, 29*(1), 4–15. Retrieved from http://edu312spring13.pbworks.com/w/file/fetch/64649998/Borko%26Putnam.pdf

Russell, T., & Korthagen, F. (2013). *Teachers who teach teachers: Reflections on teacher education.* Oxfordshire, United Kingdom: Routledge.

About the Editors

Caroline M. Crawford is an associate professor of Instructional Technology at the University of Houston-Clear Lake in Houston, Texas. She earned her doctoral degree in 1998, with specialization areas in instructional technology and curriculum theory, and began her tenure at the University of Houston-Clear Lake (UHCL) the same year. She is also a contributing faculty member in the Walden University Richard W. Riley College of Education and Leadership's Higher Education and Adult Learning doctoral program.

Her main areas of interest focus upon communities of learning, including communities of practice and learning in landscapes of practice, and the appropriate and successful integration of technologies into the learning environment; the learning environment may be envisioned as face-to-face, blended, and online environments, as well as microlearning deliverables.

Sandra L. Hardy, Ph.D., is an active researcher, board member, and former special education teacher. She served as teacher-induction consultant and coordinator of the after-school tutoring programs for students at risk. Dr. Hardy taught G.E.D. courses and served as adjunct faculty in the graduate program for teachers and administrators where she taught advanced educational psychology. She serves as vice president to the board of the Science Center and is very active in animal rescue efforts.

Dr. Hardy is a long-time member of the Association of Teacher Educators, and continues to be involved with the organization's efforts to support teachers and administrators locally, statewide, nationally, and internationally at all levels and stages of their professional development continuum. Sandra's research interests include induction, learning communities of practice, and professional development involving professional development organizations, P-12, and higher education, respectively.

About the Contributors

Louise Ammentorp, PhD, is an associate professor in the Department of Elementary and Early Childhood Education at the College of New Jersey. Her research focuses on teacher preparation and curriculum and instruction in early childhood and elementary education.

Robert Fisher is professor emeritus of curriculum and instruction at Illinois State University in Normal, Illinois, USA. His focus upon recruiting, training, and retaining superior quality classroom teachers has been a focused area of research and articulation throughout his career. Dr. Fisher's interest in the impact of classroom teachers upon the school site as well as within the community is reflected through his recent multiple year U.S. Department of Education grant *Professional Articulation for Recruiting/Retaining Teachers for Neighborhood Engagement and Renewal (PARTNER)* federally funded grant, although Dr. Fisher's grant work is extensive in nature and focused upon teacher quality.

Nancy P. Gallavan, Ph.D., is a professor of teacher education in the Department of Teaching and Learning at the University of Central Arkansas, a past president and distinguished member of the Association of Teacher Educators (ATE) and a Kappa Delta Pi (KDP) Eleanor Roosevelt Legacy Chapter inaugural member. With expertise in K-12 education, classroom assessments, curriculum development, cultural competence, social studies education, and teacher self-efficacy, Nancy is active member of AERA, ATE, KDP, NAME, and NCSS.

Contributing to more than 120 publications, Nancy has authored or coauthored *Secrets to Success for Elementary School Teachers*, *Secrets to Success for Social Studies Teachers*, *Navigating Cultural Competence: A Compass for Teachers, and Developing Performance Based Assessments* with Corwin Press, edited *Annual Editions: Multicultural Education*, editions 15, 16, and 17 with McGraw-Hill, and coedited ATE Yearbooks XIX–XXVI.

Romena M. Garrett Holbert, Ph.D., NBCT, is an associate professor at Wright State University in Dayton, Ohio, USA. Romena studies classroom community and ways of developing effective learning environments for children and adults. Her work with the Standards for Teacher Educators began during her classroom teaching when she served as a cooperating teacher and mentor. Romena serves as the chairperson of the Association of Teacher Educators (ATE) Task Force for Standards for Teacher Educators.

Benjamin R. Wellenreiter is a middle-level social studies teacher at Morton Junior High School, Morton, Illinois. Ben is also an adjunct faculty member in the Educational Studies Department at Illinois Wesleyan University, teaching courses in social studies methodology and middle-school philosophy. His research interests include adolescent socialization processes, school authority structures, patriotism education, and social studies education.

www.ingramcontent.com/pod-product-compliance
Lightning Source LLC
Chambersburg PA
CBHW030116010526
44116CB00005B/278